BELONGING

CREATING COMMUNITY
in the CLASSROOM

Mona Hajjar Halaby

BROOKLINE BOOKS • CAMBRIDGE, MA

Library of Congress Cataloging-In-Publication-Data

Halaby, Mona
    Belonging: creating community in the classroom/Mona Hajjir Halaby.
    p.cm.
Includes bibliographical references.
ISBN 1-57129-084-2
1. Classroom environment – Social aspects. 2. Caring in children. 3. Interpersonal relations. I. Title: Creating a sense of community in the classroom. II. Title.
LB3013.H32 2000
372.15–dc21

                                                                00-010675
                                                                CIP

10 9 8 7 6 5 4 3 2 1

cover illustration and design by Nathan Budoff

Published by
BROOKLINE BOOKS, INC.
P.O. Box 381047
Cambridge, Massachusetts 02238-1047
ORDER TOLL-FREE: 1-800-666-BOOK

*To my mother, Zakia Jabre Hajjar and my father,
Jean Hajjar, for giving me life and love.*

To Rahma, my nanny, for feeding me stories.

*And to Francoise Dolto, who taught me
how to listen to children.*

Contents

In Appreciation

I would like to thank the following people for their encouragement and support during the writing of *Belonging: Creating Community in the Classroom*.

I begin by thanking my husband and best friend, David, who listened to me read my early drafts, and admired them even when they were still rough and awkward. David spent many weekends alone at the movies while I sat at home writing and rewriting my manuscript. I am blessed to have his love in my life.

I also want to thank my three children, Jason, Lex and Greg who were my first teachers in understanding young children. I am grateful for all the times they spent at our family dinner table listening to my classroom stories, and giving me advice.

I am blessed to have a friend and colleague like Jill Alban who believed in me and my work. For five years Jill faithfully sat on the periphery of my class meetings, taking notes, and providing me with her keen observations, reflections and insights. Jill and I have continued to work together as we present class meeting workshops to elementary school teachers. What a gift it has been to have that kind of investment from someone so talented.

I have been fortunate enough to have colleagues who were willing to experiment with my ideas in their classrooms, so I could test them in other settings, and with students of various ages. I would like to thank Monica Grycz, Aggie Brenneman, Bob Rolling, Suzie McLean, Elyata Davis, John Marlin, Chris Engemann, Christine Julian, Jenny Bissel, Juanita Rynerson, Diane Meltzer, and Christine Duggan. I also remember the support and cherish the memory of Diane Lohman who opened her classroom to me, and who encouraged me to pursue my endeavors.

I thank my fellow writer, mentor and friend, Vivian Gussin Paley for sharing her wisdom, and for her confidence in me. I am richer from knowing her, and feel honored that she took the time to read my manuscript and write the preface. I couldn't ask for a better colleague and friend.

I am blessed to have friends who are competent writers, and who took the time to read parts of my manuscript and give me wise suggestions about its shape. I thank my friend and fellow writer, Elizabeth Fishel, who took the time to counsel me during the often grueling, yet rewarding process of finding a publisher. Her generosity of heart never ceases to astound me. As for Julie Chagi, I remember her visit to our sailboat anchorage the summer the idea for this book germinated. Her enthusiasm was the first concrete encouragement that this book needed to be published. Over the years Julie has line-edited several chapters of my book while asking me pertinent and probing questions that helped clarify my own thinking. My friend, Judy Hart, is not with us today to see my book in print, however, I still hear her excited voice, and remember our long evening talks about our writings.

I also owe thanks to Elizabeth Knoll who was the first to see the potential in my work, and who helped me tighten up my writing. I benefitted tremendously from working with her.

Thanks, also, to the friends and professionals who have shown an interest in my book, and whose assistance and support were critical: Ann Parker, Linda Cozzarelli, Mervin Freedman, Michelle Sherry, Linda Bernard, and Helen Neville. Their friendship sustained me throughout the long and often lonely journey of being a writer.

Fortunately, I have worked in environments that celebrated my success and supported my burgeoning ideas. To that regard I thank Jane Bowyer, Chair of the Department of Education at Mills College, Joan Henry, former Director of the Children's School Laboratory at Mills, Tom Little, Director of Park Day School in Oakland, Joan Serin, Special Day Teacher, and the team of teachers at Marin School, in Albany, for trusting my vision, and empowering me to become an agent of change.

I wish to thank Milton Budoff, publisher at Brookline Books, for his vision and commitment to publishing my manuscript. Milton knew clearly what this manuscript needed, and under his astute guidance I designed my final chapter, rethought drafts, and revised ideas.

And finally, this book wouldn't be here without my students who week after week opened up their hearts at our class meetings. They taught me about courage, honesty, directness, friendship, and the importance of being "real." Thank you for being my best teachers.

Preface

The seven- to ten-year-olds we are about to encounter are actors in a class-room story of theatrical dimensions. The stage business seems simple enough: children enter complaints about one another into a communal notebook, then come together every Friday to plead their cases. The plot that develops, however, captures our attention with remarkable intensity.

What is extraordinary about Mona Halaby's weekly class meeting is its emergence, for the children and teacher alike, as a source of self-knowledge and group empathy, much as the characters in a good novel come to understand each other in terms of the upheavals they cause.

Under Ms. Halaby's respectful and intuitive direction, what might otherwise be seen as petty annoyances and troublesome behaviors of ordinary schoolchildren become the high drama of young people seeking every measure of fairness and security in a community that is learning to be more trustworthy. As we come to know the children through their complaints and defenses—and the teacher through her gentle questioning—we find hidden in each session clues to an unrealized human potential. We begin to see how the young can learn to live together in harmony and dignity.

The key word is dignity, and herein lies the power of Ms. Halaby's class meeting. It is no small matter to preserve the dignity of those who misbehave, and make it clear that the group, too, must continue to support its members no matter what they are perceived to have done. The more common practice is to assign blame and let the group feel vindicated. This wise teacher, however, is willing to allow children the rare privilege of discovering for themselves something about the nature of their present unhappiness and accept responsibility for helping to create a kinder society.

These are difficult goals, but the author is not impatient for results. She accepts the subtleties of the learning process and knows that no change can take place in the moral environment of the classroom unless each child feels listened to and understood. She herself has a story to tell, and her vivid childhood memories enter the mixture of sympathetic images out of which a more realistic view of the human condition may evolve.

Perhaps the most encouraging aspect of this inspiring and instructive book is how eagerly the boys and girls reach for an opportunity to promote each other's self control and judicious spirit. We are grateful to Mona Halaby for showing them and us the way. In her class meetings, she demonstrates a model of enormous good sense and sensitivity as she builds a school society based on mutual trust and good will.

Vivian Gussin Paley

Children tend not to say what we want to hear when we want to hear it, but to the patient, perceptive adult who takes them seriously, their words are eloquent, disturbing, transforming.

Katherine Paterson

The fundamental law of human beings is interdependence.
A person is a person through other persons.

Archbishop Desmond Tutu

Introduction

Jack and Robbie ran away from our classroom on the second day of school. Five minutes later they were found hiding at the bottom of the stairwell. "I didn't know it wasn't okay to leave the classroom," said Robbie with a triumphant smile, and denying any responsibility.

It hadn't been a major offense, just a bit of mischief on their part, but it left me feeling shaken. After all, it had only been the second day of school, and I began to worry about what might be in store for that year!

"Jack, Robbie, it just wasn't safe. That's all there is to it!"

Later in the day, I brought up their little indiscretion to the class in the hopes of engaging the group in a discussion.

"Children, today Jack and Robbie ran away from the classroom, and hid under the staircase. I was worried about their safety. Can someone guess why I would have been worried?"

The children had a good idea about safety and responsibility. They gave many examples of emergencies, and the need to be supervised by a teacher.

"Your parents send you to school every morning expecting you'll be safe in my care. I have a big responsibility. When you leave the classroom without informing me, you run the risk of not being safe. Under the staircase might be the worse place to be in the event of a disaster. Do you understand what I'm saying? This is serious."

The children understood, but Jack was annoyed. He made soft whistling sounds.

At the end of the day, as I was dismissing everyone, he approached me. "You didn't have to tell everyone!" he snarled.

"Jack, once you start going to school, you become a public figure with responsibilities to the whole group. When you ran away, it affected all of us."

• • •

School brings children into their first social world. The incident with Jack made me ask myself, how does the troubled child affect the rest of the class by disrupting, clowning, withdrawing, or hurting other children? How could I help my students develop an understanding of their classmates with special needs? And how could I incorporate the children whose personal issues refuse to stay home, but rear up and affect their school behavior and the rest of the class?

The next day we gathered on the rug for our first class meeting, and to begin to define class community.

"It's like a family," said Ben.

"A community is when everyone helps each other," said Kate. "You know, like they're nice to each other, and stuff like that."

"My mom says our church is a community, 'cause everybody knows each other," said Nicko.

"Well, this year we're going to become a class community," I said. "We're going to care about each other, and help each other. We'll also learn how to solve our own problems and treat each other well. It's what Nicko said about his church. We, too, will have to learn about each other, if we're to become a community."

The next day the children were invited to bring three items from home: something special that they've been collecting, a photo album, and a favorite book. This was how we spent our first week together—sprawled on the rug, gathered around the tables, sharing our collections, talking, admiring and reading passages from our favorite books.

We discovered Jack loved baseball, Kate's Aunt Doris was in the hospital, Pasong had ten soccer trophies, Heather took ballet lessons, and William got a new yellow lab which he named Vanilla.

I, too, brought my treasures—my polished rock collection, pictures of my three sons, and a tattered copy of *Little Women*. This was how the links got formed in my classroom early in the year, so that by the end of each day we left school carrying with us the stories and mental pictures of our new friends. This was how we started to care about one another. And we were going to need that kind of caring and intimacy in order to get through the rough times ahead. Because there would be rough times, as there are in every classroom in the world—the name calling, the incessant teasing, the cheating, the punching, and of course, the hurt feelings.

Once a week our life in third grade is punctuated by a gathering on the rug to discuss the children's friendships, their quarrels, and hurts. Children want to belong and have friends. It is not their spelling tests or multiplication tables that count for them, but "Who will be my friend?" and "Who will play with me?"

At class meetings my students, who are seven through ten years old, see the cause and effect of their actions, because their conflicts are named, and there are public repercussions for their actions. The child who feels terrorized by an impulsive classmate will feel protected because he has written about his worries in the class notebook, and is then able to discuss his worries at the meeting where he will be heard by his peers. All the members of the classroom begin to feel safe, because they are seen and recognized as members of a classroom community.

Our weekly class meetings cement us together while giving everyone a place among the group. We vent our angry feelings; we support a friend; we laugh and cry. It's where we become accountable for our actions, because our actions are made public. Nothing gets swept under the rug. Anonymity is not allowed.

Through class meetings children begin to realize the class believes in their capacity to change, and trusts them in the face of adversity. The first step is seeing how they affect others, then comes taking responsibility for their actions, and finally, wanting desperately enough to be a part of our classroom community that they are willing to take the risk of changing.

The only two things I know about teaching, are that, one, change cannot occur in isolation. In order for children to feel supported, the whole class, not just their teacher, must be cheering for them, and believing that transformations can occur.

And two, classroom power has to be shared among its members. Children are more likely to change if they're included in the process of running the classroom, and making decisions. They won't change because their parents think they need to, or to please their teachers. They change because they believe there is something in it for them. They want to have friends. They want to belong.

At the beginning of the year, Jack hadn't expected his actions to be broadcast to his peers, and scrutinized by all. What might have appeared to him and others as public and exposing, slowly becomes a safe harbor, an open classroom where nothing is hidden. Being brave, having the courage to admit to some wrongdoing, telling the truth instead of lying, are all encouraged and praised publicly.

• • •

I will tell you four stories. The first one is the story of Pasong, a fiery child from Thailand who learned how to control his temper and take responsibility for his actions. The second story is about Molly whose mother was diagnosed with breast cancer, and how Molly's fear of losing her affected all of us. The third story is about Jack, the class clown, the child with learning difficulties, the outsider. And finally, the fourth child is Shireen, the bristly child of color who desperately wanted to belong, but couldn't integrate herself to the group.

This is the story of their obstinacy, their courage, their rage, their honesty, and awkward attempts at being included. And of course, it is my story, too, the story of my class as I chronicle our year together, the story of the hazards and marvels of getting close to children like Pasong, Molly, Jack, and Shireen.

To protect the confidentiality of my students, I have changed their names and the details of their lives, disguising them and their families, so that they will be unrecognizable, except possibly to themselves. The four case studies I share are for illustrative purposes only, and are sometimes compounds of various children's stories. I hope that if readers recognize themselves, they will feel I have been true to them and will not feel exposed.

The last section of the book is a Postscript in which I explain step by step how to facilitate class meetings for the teachers interested in instituting them in their own classrooms.

It is through the daily living together, the embracing of every single child in the classroom that we can become a community. The misfits, the marginal characters who hover at the periphery of the class, find a new place among the group, because class meetings give everyone a voice, and teach us how to listen to one another. Everyone is of value. Everyone is heard with respect. It is the moment, weekly, when we put away our books and papers to gather on the rug and learn how to live together.

CHAPTER ONE

Taking Responsibility

I Don't Know Why

"Pasong was pushing out the chairs when I was pushing them in."

— Joseph

At times it is hard to say why some children are liked by their peers. But not Joseph. It was obvious from the start and to all, that he was a good friend—kind, loyal and fair. Ebony curls covered his head, and thick dark eyelashes framed his brown eyes. Even though he was one of the youngest boys at school, he was one of the most agile and athletic. Driving the soccer ball down the field with ease and precision, he seemed to skim the grass.

Joseph's best friend was Pasong, short for Pasongsith, one of the oldest children in the class, and most admired among the boys. They respected his athletic agility, and were charmed by his gregarious nature. He came from Thailand, with skin chocolate brown, and straight black hair that hung down his forehead, and cut precisely above his small perky eyes.

Joseph followed Pasong everywhere like a puppy, and Pasong needed Joseph's steadfastness and loyalty.

In my classroom, the children sit at tables in groups of four. Every child has a responsibility: distributing supplies, pushing the chairs in, delivering work, or managing tables. Everyone rotates jobs, and once a month, the table configurations change to give the children a chance to get to know each other better, and to sit in different spots. It so happened that Joseph and Pasong were sitting at the same table. I like to seat two friends together at the beginning of the year in order to help children feel more at ease.

Joseph was responsible for pushing the chairs in, while Pasong was in charge of distributing supplies. Knowing how conscientious Joseph was, I knew he must have felt concerned by this altercation with Pasong, because it prevented him from doing his job at his table.

At the meeting, after flipping the hourglass for our traditional one minute of silence and transition, I read Joseph's entry to the children huddled around me on the rug.

"Joseph, tell us more about this incident," I asked.

He hesitated as he eyed Pasong with an apologetic glance. Everyone was quiet, knowing that it took a lot of courage to write about one's best friend, and to expose him publicly. We all knew to wait.

Finally Joseph spoke. Every time he did his job pushing the chairs in, Pasong would go around undoing it for what appeared to be no good reason. I asked Joseph whether he had expressed his frustration to Pasong before our meeting. He answered yes. Then his voice cracked as he turned to Pasong,

"Why did you keep on doing it, even after I said to stop? I didn't like it."

Pasong looked contrite, but couldn't speak. I asked him gently, "Pasong, do you remember what happened?" He nodded. "Tell us from your perspective what happened at your table."

I tried to keep a non-judgmental tone of voice as I spoke. Class meeting is not a court hearing where children are convicted of crimes. The emphasis is on telling one's story from one's own point of view, in order to see that situations or events could be perceived differently depending on one's vantage point.

At Artist Workshop we were studying perspective. The children were looking at drawings of the same house, but from different perspectives—aerial views, side views, back views. The house looked different in each drawing, yet it was always the same old house.

"The problems we bring to class meetings are like the house," I had said to the class. "But each one of us sees it from a different perspective."

Pasong's eyes darted around, checking the room for accusatory gazes or ridicule. Yet, the class was poised in silence.

"I don't know why I did it." He paused, looking gloomy. "Sorry, Joseph. I won't give you any more trouble with the chairs," he added while vigorously rubbing his knees with the palms of his hands. Joseph nodded nervously, then took a deep breath that felt as though it had been compressed inside his chest for a long, long time.

"Thank you, Joseph, for sharing your problem with us," I said. "It was brave of you to take the risk of speaking up against a friend. You stayed true to your feelings, even if that meant embarrassing Pasong. As for you, Pasong, thank you for your courage to be honest, and for apologizing to Joseph. You did it on your own. That's when it really counts. It takes a great person to do that. Does anyone else want to add anything?"

No one did. Maybe they were still a bit shy. After all, this was only the second class meeting of the year.

Pasong did keep his promise. He never bothered Joseph with the chairs again.

Whose Child Was He After All?

Never had we had so many entries in our class notebook than the second week of October. Twenty-one problems in all. What was wrong with my class? Did I have the most challenging group of kids on the planet, or was it me? Maybe by offering them this notebook and class meetings, I'd created a class of complainers and tattlers.

Pasong's name appeared in a number of problems, and he had written a few of them himself.

The night before our meeting, I fantasized calling in sick. I didn't want to do these class meetings. It was getting too hard. But if I weren't there to facilitate them, they'd have to be postponed to the following Friday, the agenda doubling in size. No escape. So the next day I braced myself and went to school.

Shireen was a large black girl with a big round face. She spoke in a soft high-pitched voice as though she were a baby trapped in an oversized body. It was difficult for her to play with other children for more than ten minutes without a tearful confrontation. Unfortunately, I never saw the beginning, or could prevent the explosion. It was only when the tears were being shed that I was called in.

That day at class meeting, I asked Shireen to choose only one from her six problems, the most pressing one. This is what she chose:

> "Pasong was sticking his tongue out at me. He said he wished that I did not go to this school, and he said he wished I was dead. Outside he started to tease me. I said stop, but he kept on doing it. He called me the fat girl at school. He also called me a jerk. He said I'm so fat that I will turn into a pig. He keeps on calling me names."
>
> — Shireen

We were all shocked. No one in our class had ever been attacked with such cruelty. I had a hard time believing that Pasong could be capable of such viciousness. Was Shireen lying about him just to get our attention? Since she had not been getting along with anyone else at school, I wondered about the extent of her responsibility in the matter.

"Shireen, tell us what's been happening between you and Pasong."

"Well, you see," Shireen, composed, spoke softly, her eyes cast down. "He's been mean to me, calling me names all the time."

"Did you get a chance to tell him how that made you feel?"

"No," she whispered.

"Tell him now. He's right here. It's important he hears you say how you feel."

As she lifted her eyes, her gaze turned slowly to Pasong. He was playing nervously with the cord around the hood of his sweatshirt.

"I didn't like it when you called me these names," she said. "It hurt my feelings."

Her voice was subdued; it didn't contain the force of her meaning. This discrepancy made her language unreal. Why couldn't she express herself freely to Pasong in front of the class? She had been hurt by his insults, yet her voice and body language didn't look pained or angry. I even thought I saw a slight Cheshire-cat grin on her face. Was she pleased to see Pasong squirming at the meeting? Or was it hard for her to express negative feelings in public?

Pasong's face was tight and his eyes glowed with tears. "Pasong, why don't you tell us what happened for you?"

I was expecting to hear a counter-attack, or even some heart-felt denials with examples of being teased by Shireen, anything but the silence that followed. Pasong looked down at his sneakers.

Shireen couldn't restrain her feelings any longer. She stared at him with eyes filled with venom. "You called me all these mean names, like fat girl, and that I'll turn into a pig, but why, why?"

"I don't know why," answered Pasong, his face still down, his voice cracking.

I wanted to bellow, 'How can you not know? That's unacceptable!' Instead, I said, "Pasong, look at Shireen's face. Look at how sad she is right now."

"I'm sad, too," he unexpectedly poured out his grief. He wept as he told us he'd been having nightmares every night, nightmares about his birth mother. He was worried about her, because he had heard she was sick. His adoptive parents were still in contact with her, and she occasionally wrote to him.

The class knew Pasong had been adopted from Thailand at age six. In fact, in September, the first time Pasong talked about his birth parents, he told us they had been shot by soldiers. Since at the time I had not had all the details on his adoption, I decided to meet with his adoptive parents to hear the whole story.

They told me that Pasong had been a street child in Bangkok, raised in poverty in a small aluminum-covered shack. His birth mother, Noy, had nine children, and no reliable man around. But it was with the older boys from the neighborhood that Pasong hung around, living in the streets from dawn to midnight, scavenging, stealing, doing mischief.

"Pasong told us that his birth parents had been shot by soldiers," I said to his parents. "Is that what he believes is the reason he was adopted?"

George, Pasong's gentle, soft-spoken father, answered, "No, Pasong knows his mother's alive, and that she's too poor to take care of him. He doesn't know his father."

"But why didn't he tell us the truth?" I asked.

"He told you they were dead, because he needs to fabricate a story he can live with, a heroic story. He can't tolerate the idea that children lose their parents, unless the parents are dead." After adopting Pasong and Toon, Pasong's younger brother, George and Karen had spent many hours talking to a social worker who specialized in adoption cases.

Now at our class meeting there was no fantasy. At age eight, Pasong understood the reality of his situation. He could talk about his birth mother, and have her be alive elsewhere, away from him, yet still alive. The point he had trouble with was figuring out whose child he was. One time he told us that his mother, Noy, had nine children, including himself, then he corrected his statement, "Well, I'm not really her child." Was he Noy's son back in Thailand, or Karen's here in Oakland?

"Pasong," I asked, "would you like to write a letter to your birth mother today? Would that make you feel closer to her?"

"Yes," he answered, "and maybe the other kids can draw her some pictures. She can't speak English, but she can read their names."

Then he looked worried. "I have one little question," he added. "What if she dies before she gets my letter?"

"You know, it's natural to worry about losing the people we love. But I bet your birth mother will receive your letter, and she'll be fine, you'll see." I paused. "Maybe it's hard for you to play nicely with the other children when you have worries inside you, when you're frightened, or angry, or sad."

He nodded, even though I doubted he understood what I was saying.

"But you know, Pasong, coming back to Shireen's problem in the notebook, it's not okay to be mean to other children, and hurt them because you're hurting inside. It doesn't give you the right."

"Yes, Mona," he whispered, his eyes to the floor.

"Pasong," I added, "I have something near my bed that I call my dream journal. It's a blank book in which I write my dreams when I wake up in the morning. Sometimes when the dream is especially scary, it helps me to put it into words. Would you like your own dream journal that you can keep here in class?"

His face lit up, "Yes!" he exclaimed. I had had an intuition that he needed a gift, an offering in the bleakness of this moment.

"And you can write in it when you come to school if you've had a bad dream the night before. Maybe if you put down all those scary images onto paper, then you won't have to create them in class among your friends. What do you think?"

"I can try, Mona," he said.

"That's the best any of us can do, Pasong."

"Shireen? Pasong?" I asked, "Is there anything else either one of you wants to say?"

"No," they replied together.

Even though the problem was written by Shireen, we had spent almost the entire time on Pasong. Intuitively, I felt he needed our attention. As for Shireen, she seemed all right at the moment, although I had concerns about her.

It would have been nice had Pasong apologized to her, but I've made it a point never to force apologies from children, because they can apologize only when they truly feel enough empathy for one another.

Pasong was enclosed in his own world of pain and anger. I couldn't ask him to feel for Shireen too, not yet.

Hero or Tyrant?

Pasong could kick, catch, aim, bat, run, jump, dodge, he could do anything on the sports field, except be a good friend. That was his Achilles tendon. Early in the year everyone wanted to be on his team, but starting in November, two short entries by Ben began to mar Pasong's reputation:

> "Whenever we make one mistake in baseball, Pasong yells at us."
>
> — Ben

> "When someone from the opposing team scores a goal, Pasong yells at our goalie."
>
> — Ben

Who was Ben? An only child, precocious and bright, living in the world of adults, talking like them. Only his pudgy hamster-like cheeks and slight lisp reminded me that he was seven years old. Although Ben excelled in every academic subject, he could barely stand or walk without tripping. He resembled a marionette whose threads would suddenly go from tight to loose, forcing him to tumble from his chair to the floor. Ben did not create these distractions as a class clown, but rather from poor muscle tone which he exercised weekly in occupational therapy. The children never made fun of his clumsiness.

So what does it mean when a child like Ben complains about the most coordinated student in our class? Was it about Ben's envy of Pasong's ease on the soccer field, or was the latter truly abusing his power?

I remembered a class meeting early in September when Nicko lashed out at Pasong, "You act like you're the boss when we play baseball." Now it was Ben's turn to accuse Pasong.

At our class meeting, I read Ben's entries to the class. Pasong appeared distracted and removed. Ben, on the other hand, lunged fast as though he had rehearsed his lines, and needed to recite them quickly before forgetting them.

"Pasong gets so mad whenever our goalie doesn't block the ball in time. I mean, it's really not always our fault, you know. He starts to yell at the goalie, and then he stomps away. Come on, we can't always catch the ball when it's coming our way." Words came easily to Ben.

"What happens for you at sports," I asked Pasong.

He was still. Only his eyes roamed around the room.

I said gently, "So, tell us, Pasong, what do you remember happened?"

He took a deep breath and spoke slowly. Now his eyes were glued to the rug. "I don't know...I mean, I don't remember."

"Is this hard for you?"

He nodded. Ben waved his hand impatiently.

"Ben, I'd like Pasong to have a turn and respond to you before you add something else," I said.

He accepted reluctantly. He was not used to waiting. He loved to talk. It had taken me months to teach him to raise his hand rather than call out in class.

"Pasong, what do you mean when you say you can't remember?"

"I just don't remember yelling. I mean, sometimes I get excited during the game, but...but...I don't remember yelling at the goalie."

"Can you see how dangerous it is not to know or remember what we did? I mean, without that knowledge, we can never go back to examine the reasons for our behavior, and when we can't examine, we stop growing and learning. Can you see that? Do you know what I'm saying?"

I thought I might have lost Pasong with my psychological speech, but he was listening intently.

"You see, Pasong, when you've got lots of power, you become responsible for others. You need to treat them well. In order to be a good leader you've got to include your friends in the process of decision-making. That's what a good president does, that's what a good teacher does."

Time to involve the whole group. "Tell me, children, what are the qualities you look for in good leaders?"

"They're nice to you."

"They're fair when there's a problem."

"They listen to you."

"They don't boss you around all the time."

I hadn't planned on shifting to a childhood anecdote, but I trusted my intuition.

"You know, as I'm listening to what you're saying, I'm reminded of a story that happened to me when I was in fourth grade..."

"Oh, goodie, a Mona story!" the children interjected. They loved hearing about my childhood. All of a sudden, I became their age. I was one of them, someone with little power in the world of adults.

"Yes, well, when I was in fourth grade, there was a girl in our class who was very pretty, and wore stylish clothes..."

"What was her name?" Erin called out.

Erin was always preoccupied with clothes, making friends, and being fashionable.

"Marianne," I answered, "and everyone wanted to be Marianne's friend. Everyone begged to sit with her at lunch. Everyone wanted to invite her to play after school. But you know what? She could be mean. She'd say you were her friend one day, but then the next day she'd refuse to include you in her games, and you'd feel left out and foolish. You didn't know whether she was lying, forgetting, or breaking her promises. Marianne used to be the most popular girl in fourth grade, until we stopped trusting her, and eventually we lost interest in her."

"So what happened to her?" asked Sofia.

"Oh! It took some time, but she changed. She realized she lost all of her friends and felt lonely."

"It's kind of like the story of the boy who cried wolf. People stopped believing him," said Molly.

"Do you think it's easy to be popular?" I asked.

Loud no's thundered in the room.

"Some of you seem to know about being popular. What does it feel like?" I asked.

William spoke first. "I know I'm kind of good at sports." He smiled shyly. "And the kids like it when I'm on their team. That makes me feel good."

"Thank you, William."

Sanford, a younger boy who had moved into our class mid-year, raised his hand.

"In my other class I knew I was popular, 'cause I made kids laugh. You know, I would say jokes, silly things like that. I know kids liked it."

"Thanks, Sanford."

"I know Latoya was, like, popular when she was at our school," said Erin. "Like, you know, she was everybody's friend."

I noticed that Pasong didn't share his own experience of being popular. Perhaps he wasn't aware of the powerful magnetism that had drawn the boys to him.

Our time was almost up. "You know, children, I'm glad Ben wrote up his problem in the notebook, because we started to discuss what it means to have power and be popular. This was a very important meeting."

Ben, who at the beginning of the meeting had been rearing to lash out at Pasong, had remained silent the rest of the time. I knew that it would not have served our purpose to dwell on the particulars of Pasong's behavior at sports. The discussion we had instead, about leadership and popularity, was much more useful to everyone. Ben was heard, and Pasong warned.

Now my role was to observe more closely what went on during lunch and recess. Waiting doesn't come easily, especially to teachers and parents who feel compelled to solve the problems that create mayhem in their environments. There was a time in my teaching career when I thought I was meant to rescue my students, and solve their problems with speed. If I couldn't do it immediately, I felt incompetent and inefficient. Now I've learned to hold myself back, to slow down a bit and wait.

Three months later

Pasong's problems escalated in frequency and severity. By February, we had pages of entries, not only by Ben, but also by Jeremiah, Tim, Joseph, Nicko, Robbie, all of them complaining about Pasong's conduct at sports:

"Pasong cheated when we were playing three flies up. He kept passing the ball to William. We never got a fly."

"At soccer Pasong grabbed my shirt and pushed me."

"Pasong said I couldn't be the pitcher at lunch recess. It wasn't fair that Nicko got to be the pitcher for the whole game."

"Pasong was calling me a bad thrower. I told him I didn't like that, but he said 'You're no good.'"

"When we were playing soccer, Pasong tripped me on purpose."

"In hockey I said 'Good game' to Pasong, and he said 'Shut up.'"

Nobody wanted to be on Pasong's team anymore; no one wanted to be pushed around, insulted, mistreated. Pasong, once the most popular boy on the field, had lost his power.

At the meeting I read the litany of accusations, and asked Pasong to explain his behavior.

"I don't know," he answered.

I didn't have to respond. Joseph, discarding his allegiance to his friend, jumped in with fury, "That's what you always say." Then he proceeded to mimic Pasong's voice, "'I don't know, I don't know, I don't remember.' Well, we can't believe you anymore."

Pasong's cheeks turned crimson. His nostrils flared. Silent tears slid down his face.

Oh, no, could I have prevented Pasong's humiliation? Did I set him up for failure? No, I thought. I had given him opportunities to change. I had told him about his responsibility as a leader, about listening to his friends, about Marianne who lost her popularity.

Pasong had had his chances, I reminded myself. Some people learn from these chances, others don't. In that moment I realized he needed more than second chances, he needed something else.

Instituting special contracts to improve students' behavior had always sounded punitive and behavioristic to me. It hadn't been my style. I was sure the children could change when they realized that I trusted them, and that they belonged to a caring community. Usually I was right. However, today as I faced Pasong's silent tears, and the class's rage, I knew the time was ripe for instituting a self-governing contract for him. I looked at him, and spoke slowly for emphasis, pausing after every statement to give it importance and weight.

"Pasong, the children are angry and frustrated. Too many people have been hurt in our class. We can't create a community when there's so much pain and violence. Talking at class meetings, writing in the notebook, having a dream journal, all these things didn't help enough."

I took a deep breath and continued.

"I've read in a book that sometimes what really helps a student change his behavior is a self-governing contract. I'd like us to try it. Here is how it works: You and I decide together on a school activity that means a lot to you. Then the next time you hurt someone's feelings, body or property, you have to give up the activity you've selected."

Someone asked, "What does 'self-governing' mean?" I explained that it meant 'being in charge.' Pasong was going to be in charge of changing his behavior.

I continued detailing the contract for Pasong and the class. "Step one means you miss the activity you selected once. If you hurt someone again, you move to step two – you miss your favorite activity twice in a row. If you hurt someone again, it's step three—and you miss a week's worth of your favorite activity."

I stopped briefly to gauge my audience.

"Pasong, do you understand the seriousness of this?"

"Yes, Mona." He seemed earnest. Then, almost immediately, his face lit up. "Oh, it's easy for me to decide on my favorite activity! You know what it is, don't you? It's sports!"

"Yes, you know yourself well!" I said. "First infraction you'll miss one day of sports. Second infraction you'll miss two days of sports, and third infraction you'll miss the two days of sports, plus all the recesses of that week."

He looked a bit overwhelmed as he heard the references to sports and recess. His friends looked equally crushed. This was Big Time.

"So next time someone bothers you, you can say, 'I don't like it,' or you can write it up in the notebook, but it's not acceptable to clobber someone or call someone names. You're getting older now, you've got to take responsibility for your actions."

Ben asked, "What if Pasong does it a fourth time? What then?"

"After step three, he gets a clean slate and starts fresh at step one again."

Someone asked, "Will Pasong have to be on the self-governing contract every time someone writes him up in the notebook?"

"Oh, no," Nina quickly replied with a knowing grin. She was well beyond her years. "That would make it too easy for kids in the class to get Pasong in trouble on purpose."

"Yes, Nina, you're right. I'm the one who decides whether the problem is serious enough to activate the contract."

I didn't want Pasong's classmates to leave the meeting thinking, 'Well, that's his problem. I've got nothing to do with it.' We all affect each other for better or worse. So before dismissing the class, I added, "Children, we're all going to work together, because if Pasong fails at his contract, that means we've all failed to support him. But if he succeeds, then we've all succeeded in creating a caring community."

"Also, if anyone of you would like a contract to change something you don't like about yourself, let me know. I've heard of kids who wanted to complete their homework every week, or come to school on time. They choose a contract to help them change. You think about it, and let me know if you're interested."

I didn't expect any takers just then, but I wanted the children to see that they could be in charge of making changes in their lives, and have some control over their behavior.

The next day I typed Pasong's contract. He and I signed it, and dated it. Then he passed it around to his classmates to sign. He smiled as he went around the tables in our classroom soliciting signatures. I heard Joseph cheer him on, "You can do it, Pasong!"

Pasong took the contract home for his parents to sign. They promised to give him the support he needed to be successful, and they were anxious to see him learn how to use some self-control.

Pasong's story is the uphill climb some children have to undertake, not by choice, but because of their personality, their history, their circumstances. I knew that his complicated history which included poverty, abandonment, and adoption had to account for his difficulties at school. However, by the end of the school year, he was seen as someone who had the potential to change, someone who could be trusted.

Over the next few months I had to activate Pasong's contract four times, and after that, never again. I'm not sure though that these changes affected his life outside our classroom door. I gathered from his parents and his *After School* teachers that he continued to have conflicts with his peers. Maybe he could make these changes only in my classroom because some limits had been clearly set for him, and because there were predictable consequences. Even though I had initially not been comfortable with the idea of a contract, Pasong taught me that to reach different children, I need to travel different paths.

The Words to Say It

"Pasong was saying things about girls and teasing us. He was making faces, too."

— Nina and Lauren

Nina spoke first. "I just didn't like it how Pasong made faces at us, puckering his lips like that." She demonstrated with her eyes tightly shut in an exaggerated amorous way. Some of the boys giggled. It was spring time. Many teachers attest to a certain romantic quality floating in the air.

"It's not funny," snapped Molly.

Everyone was a little testy, embarrassed, ill at ease, everyone, that is, except for Pasong who seemed quite satisfied with the splash of emotions this entry had brought about.

Lauren, one of the youngest girls in the class, added, "Also Pasong said that girls are stupid, and I didn't like that."

This was the first time Lauren had spoken at our meetings. Even though she usually appeared mousy, today she had the strength to stand up to Pasong.

"Pasong, what do you remember happened?"

No response.

"Pasong, two girls in our class have hurt feelings, what are we going to do about it?"

"I was mad. That's all!" he barked, obviously annoyed at my persistence.

Nicko who had a short fuse, turned to Pasong. "Take it out on yourself, not on someone else!"

Nicko reminded me of a stocky little Leprechaun. Round face sprinkled with freckles, topped with a thick mop of red hair. He and Pasong were magnetic friends—attracting and repelling.

I wondered what direction to take. This issue didn't seem to be about boy-girl trouble. I knew I didn't want to get sidetracked with the obvious, concrete problem, but instead follow the more subtle path that was opening up in front of me—the issue of coping under duress.

"Children, what I think I'm hearing is that sometimes we have angry feelings that get dumped on the wrong people, at the wrong time. Tell me, how do you cope when you're frustrated because something happened that had nothing to do with the people around you? How can you make sure you don't hurt others?"

"Sometimes I get really upset, so I go and punch some pillows."

"I go to my room, and have a cooling off time."

"I walk away, and, like, I try to ignore it."

"I go to the bathroom and splash cold water on my face."

"I go to my room and I, like, slam the door and I throw myself on the bed and I stay by myself until I'm, like, calm again."

"These are good suggestions. Now, Pasong, why were you mad the day you bothered the girls?"

"I don't know."

"Remember, Pasong, it's not okay anymore not to know." He remained silent, pouting.

What I was about to say was risky. "Does anyone in this class know why things might appear to be hard for Pasong?"

The children watched me with caution. Was I opening a Pandora box filled with prejudice, and discrimination? I was inviting them to name what we'd all felt, but were afraid to utter, namely that Pasong's life experiences had been difficult and different from ours. Maybe something needed to be unearthed, like a large rock half-submerged in dirt that trips you every time you walk along. Time to dig out that rock.

I continued, "We all know Pasong's generally had more trouble in our class. Why is it? It may help him understand himself better. Does anyone have an idea?" My questions invited the children to be thoughtful and supportive.

Ben spoke first. "I think Pasong has problems because he keeps being angry that he was separated from his real mom."

Then Rachel wanted to speak. "Maybe Pasong didn't have enough power about his parents. I mean he couldn't choose what he wanted to do when he got adopted."

My students were more aware of Pasong's situation than I had expected. They were able to zero in on the most vulnerable and tender issue in his life—the loss of his birth mother.

How could he trust us? All the support we gave him could not undo the anger at having been separated from his mother.

Nina raised her hand. "I guess Pasong didn't have any control in his life, so that's why he's angry about a lot of things."

"Thanks, Nina," I paused. "Pasong, what do you think? Does any of this make sense to you?"

He nodded quietly. Everyone was conscious of the weight hanging over us—the truth expressed by the children in honest, direct terms.

"But he's got to change his attitude," said Nicko who couldn't forget, Nicko who brought us back to reality.

"Yes, you're right, Nicko," I said, "Pasong needs to change. But how can you change if you're angry all the time?"

"We're nice to him, why can't he be nice to us?" asked Joseph.

"Pasong, do you have an answer to that?" I asked.

He shook his head.

If I were to have ended the meeting now, would I have been crippling Pasong, doing him a disservice by giving him allowances no one else was given?

"I understand that things have been hard for you so far, but that doesn't give you the permission to hurt other people. We need to find ways to cope with some unpleasant things in life without hurting others. You know, Pasong, no one has a perfect life. So, my wish for you, is that we can see you grow and change your attitude. We're all counting on you. The people in this class care about you."

"I know that, Mona," replied Pasong his eyes brimming with tears.

"Nina, Lauren, it wasn't right that you were teased and hurt because Pasong couldn't control his anger. Sometimes we get hurt accidentally; we happen to be at the wrong time at the wrong place. Can you see that Pasong's anger had nothing to do with you?"

"Yeah," they both answered.

"But I wish Pasong could find a good way to express his anger, so we don't get hurt again," said Nina.

"You're right. That needs to happen now. Right, Pasong?"

"Yeah," he answered softly.

Two months later

Things were becoming more clearly defined. I didn't need to be highly perceptive to sense the sexual tension in this problem:

> "We do not like it when Pasong acts like he's our boyfriend or lover. He hugs us and pats us on the back."
>
> — Nina and Kate

"Nina, tell us more about what happened."

She was trying hard to control herself, and she nodded in a business-like fashion as she took a deep breath before speaking.

"The other day I was getting some paper from the supply shelf, and Pasong came right behind me and blocked my way. I tried to slip away, but I couldn't, 'cause, you know, how it's too tight in there...well, I just didn't like what he was doing." She stopped abruptly.

"Did it make you feel trapped?" I asked.

"Yeah, I couldn't get out of there, and I could tell he was doing it on purpose. He had this big smile on his face." She closed her eyes and shook her head with aggravation.

"Kate, do you want to add something?"

"Well, Nina and I don't like how Pasong is treating us. I don't know who he thinks he is, but he's not our boyfriend or anything."

Some children covered their mouths to muffle laughter; others goggled at Pasong, arching their eyebrows. Pasong didn't know whether to laugh or cry. He knew his turn to talk was coming.

"So, Pasong, what is this about?" I asked.

He tried to legitimize his crowding Nina at the supply shelf. He claimed it was an accident. "There's no room near that shelf," he argued. He guaranteed there had been no foul play on his part.

We listened as he defended himself with rationality and poise. This was the first time Pasong had not appeared ashamed, and had not remained silent when accused. I wasn't sure what to make of it. Could the girls have misinterpreted his signals?

"Girls, I wonder whether Pasong was trying to be friends with you. Sometimes kids don't know quite how to approach others. They end up seeming awkward or making fools of themselves while attempting to make contact."

"Oh, if Pasong had wanted to be our friend, that would have been okay," said Nina. "But it wasn't like that, Mona. It was more like, like..." Her face was scrunched up as she searched for the right word. Then she popped up, her eyes like big blue marbles. "You know," she said. "It was like...like...sexual harassment."

The words tumbled out of her mouth. I braced myself in shock. How did this nine-year-old girl know to use the words to describe this particular situation? The rest of the class sat wide-eyed. Did they comprehend all this?

Tim raised his hand. I was speechless, so perhaps Tim could save me momentarily from having to respond.

Tall and pale, slow in his speech and movements, Tim was the quintessential honest, earnest child. He had been Pasong's friend since first grade. Maybe he wanted to come to Pasong's rescue.

"One time Pasong sexually abused me," said Tim with a calm that didn't match the horror of his words.

I scanned the room. Pasong's eyelids lowered, and his face which was normally expressive, became dark, twisted, distorted.

In an instant someone asked, "What do you mean?"

Tim answered, "It's when someone touches your private parts."

I had no control of this meeting. No foresight, no hindsight. No time for a plan, for a course of action. Just barreling down with speed.

Nicko wanted to speak. "Pasong tried to do that to me, too, but my dad taught me how to block anyone who wants to touch me like that." He stood up and got into a self-defense posture that protected his groin. The class watched, mesmerized.

Joseph added quickly in a baby voice, "Pasong did that to me, too." He raised his shoulders, a meek, hurt smile painted on his face.

"Pasong, what happened? Tell us about it." I wanted him to deny these accusations. I wanted him to confront the boys, and scream that they were liars, that all of this was a made-up story.

However, Pasong did not respond. He sat in a tight ball, his arms wrapped around his folded legs in front of him, rocking back and forth.

What? Had my whole class been molested? Or were the boys talking about sexual exploration? At this point, I couldn't tell the difference. Wake me up somebody, wake me up! Nothing in my teacher training classes had prepared me for this moment.

'One step at a time, Mona,' I said to myself. 'The last thing they need is a hysterical teacher. Start with some acknowledgments, some validations. You don't have to take action right away.'

"Thank you, Boys, for sharing something so private. It takes a lot of courage and a lot of trust to share your stories with the class. And I'm also very proud of the entire group for taking this topic seriously, and for discussing it together."

Talking with children about teasing, being popular, or making friends had been safe and comfortable. However, childhood molestation was another issue. Yet, I knew the greatest gift I could give them was to allow them to speak out, and break the veil of silence.

I turned to Tim. "Tim, you spoke first, tell us about it," I said with no hint of hesitance, as though molestation were the most obvious thing a child would want to talk about.

"I was playing at Pasong's house, and he touched my private parts, so I told his mom about it, and I told my mom that I didn't want to play at Pasong's house anymore." There was vigor in his voice as he spoke in one long string of words. This pale and quiet boy had bounced back.

"Joseph, what about you? Tell us some more?"

In a soft, barely perceptible voice, he replied, "I was at Pasong's house." Then he stopped to look in Pasong's direction. Was he asking permission? Then he added tentatively, "We were...uh...fooling around in his living-room on the sofa, and then he...uh...he touched my pants." Joseph's voice quivered. He stopped and looked humiliated by the words that had just slipped out of his mouth.

"Thank you, Joseph," I said. "It's hard to talk about the memories that make us uncomfortable. I understand."

I could have doubted the veracity of these stories, yet, I couldn't imagine that my students would create these scenarios for attention, or to get Pasong in trouble. What they said was too painful to be a lie. In any case, I've found out that my students don't lie to me. Sometimes they exaggerate; sometimes they belittle, but they don't lie to my face.

I turned back to Tim who seemed to be more resilient and willing to speak up. "Tim, how does all of that make you feel?"

"I don't like it!" he snapped.

I wanted him to talk to Pasong directly in order to dislodge something inside, some feelings, some words, some howls or tears, anything—anything, but this heavy silence that was punctuated by the creaking of Pasong's shoes as he rocked ceaselessly.

"Did you get a chance to let Pasong know about that?"

"No."

"Would you like to do it now?"

Tim turned around to face Pasong who was trying to make himself small and inconspicuous.

"Pasong, I didn't like it when you touched me!" Tim's voice blasted.

Pasong hung his head low.

"Did you hear Tim?" I asked.

Pasong nodded, then swung his head from left to right. A faint look of disgust crossed his face. What was that look?

He wasn't saying anything, or doing anything to save himself. I had to take the risk of throwing him a line. "Pasong, did anyone ever sexually abuse you?"

He nodded readily, as he wiped the tears.

"Was it someone from our class?" I asked, knowing full well that it couldn't be, but needing to keep him talking to me.

Pasong had always seemed to have an abundance of sexual energy and awareness, well beyond the average eight-year-old. A previous episode made sense to me now. It was earlier in the year—on class photo-taking day. We walked the children to a different building where the photographer had set up all of his equipment. Several children needed to use the bathroom. The girls went into the women's bathroom, escorted by my student teacher.

Because we didn't have a male teacher with us, no one could step into the men's bathroom to supervise the boys. Suddenly, I heard loud screams and roars of laughter from behind the door. I decided that this was the kind of emergency that warranted breaching the gender barriers. I pushed open the door and marched into the men's bathroom. Pasong was standing peeing at the urinal, his face glowing with pride and joy, his pants bunched down at his ankles, wiggling his behind to an audience of shrieking boys. I heard a distressed child complaining from the closed stall that Pasong had repeatedly crawled under the door to peek at him. I calmed down everyone, and got Pasong out of the bathroom.

As I walked out the door, I wondered why Pasong needed to invade other children's privacy and put himself on exhibit. At the time I had thought it had been a typical boyish prank or bravado. I had no indication then that Pasong had been molested, but I knew from my readings that children who experienced molestation or rape are apt to respond to sexual matters by either withdrawing, or by being prematurely interested in sex.

After the bathroom incident, I decided to keep a watchful eye on Pasong, and with his parents' permission, I invited his therapist, Hank, to come talk to our staff about the ways we could best help Pasong. Hank came to our meeting, and shared with us what he knew about Pasong's early childhood.

Pasong grew up in the streets of Bangkok in the company of older boys. He had been physically abused. Cigarette burns, like small stars were etched along his upper arms. No one knew how it had happened. As for sexual abuse, Hank didn't know; it hadn't come up in their work, but with a history and background such as Pasong's, he suspected it.

A few months later we started to notice that Pasong had an all too rich English vocabulary of sexually offensive and suggestive language. We thought that since it was in English, he must have learned it in the United States. My first instinct said he hadn't learned it at home. So, where did he pick it up from? I met with Karen, his mother, one afternoon to alert her to my concerns. Did Pasong have a male baby-sitter? Was he hanging out with teenage boys in his neighborhood? Karen admitted that he was spending considerable time after school on the street playing football with two teenage boys who lived on their block. She wasn't keen on them. They had foul mouths and were constantly yelling profanities. I suggested that Karen monitor, if not limit, Pasong's interactions with these boys. She said she would try, but that it would be hard, since Pasong idolized them.

For months I collected clues. I observed Pasong's interactions, and watched him play. Yet, there was nothing suspicious or alarming. So, when at class meetings I asked him who had sexually abused him, I listened very carefully.

"No," he answered, "it wasn't someone from our class." Pause. "It was someone from...I mean who lives in my neighborhood." He stopped to nod. "A teenager." Then Pasong looked around, almost afraid to continue, but he went on. "He pulled down my...my...my pants when he was in my backyard." He spoke seriously. I knew he was worried that someone might laugh. No one even breathed. He finished his story in one quick burst. "But my mom saw him from the window and she yelled, and he stopped and he ran away."

I was expecting a molestation story from Thailand. However, because I knew Pasong had a couple of troubled teenagers on his street, his story was believable.

"How did you feel about it, Pasong?"

"I didn't like it."

Joseph, who had had a chance to regain his dignity, burst out, "Well, then, if you didn't like it, why did you do it to us? Did you think we were gonna like it?"

"I don't know why I did it."

"Pasong, have you talked about all of this with Hank?" I asked. Everyone in our class knew Hank who had once come to visit us as Pasong's guest.

"Not much."

"I recommend you do. You need someone to help you. You got scared and you got hurt, and now you are scaring and hurting other children. It's not okay to touch other people's private parts."

I turned to the whole class. "Children, your body is your own. Don't let anyone touch you in that way. If someone tries to, yell 'No,' as loud as you can, and go tell a responsible adult who will help you. Do you understand what I'm saying?"

Affirmative. They knew. They understood. Many of them shared stories from home, warnings, precautions. Interestingly, it was mostly the girls who spoke up. Their parents had warned them. The boys listened. Do we, as parents and teachers tend to caution girls more than boys? It's good we prepare girls, but are we giving them the message that only they are vulnerable? Yet boys are just as easily the prey of a sex offender as girls are.

We ended the meeting. Everyone was somber. Perhaps a little sad. I chose not to caution the children about sharing this meeting with their families. I knew I was taking a risk. I could be alarming some parents. And what about the confidentiality around Pasong and his family? However, it was more important for the children to not be alarmed, and to feel that this meeting was no different than any previous one.

Later That Evening

That evening I informed Vince, my school principal, of the situation. He would stand by me if I needed any help. Then I reached Pasong's mother. She had known about the incident with Tim, but was devastated by the extent of the damage. I asked her to inform Hank as soon as possible. I, too, wanted to talk to him. What were the California laws regarding a child molesting another child? Did I need to report this case to Child Protection Services? And how do I handle potentially angry or frightened parents?

As I sat waiting for Hank to call me, I could feel the anxiety mounting by the hour. 'Have I harmed my students by having class meetings? Was it more than I had bargained for?' A year ago I started the meetings because I wanted the children to learn how to get along together, how to solve their problems and create a caring community. How naive of me not to have anticipated the issues that had surfaced today!

Finally Hank called. We talked on the phone for over an hour. He informed me that I didn't need to call C.P.S. Because Pasong had touched other children his age, it would be considered sexual exploration. Had Pasong touched younger children, it would have been considered coercion, thus necessitating the intervention of Protective Services. I was relieved. In addition, the fact that Pasong was in therapy was a factor in his favor.

Then Hank helped me think of ways to reassure the parents. He thought they might need to realize how valuable class meetings had been for the class. Children do not talk about private matters unless they feel perfectly safe. Hank wanted me to point out to the parents how healthy and beneficial the meetings had been for all the children, not only for the main protagonists, but for everyone, girls and boys.

The following week Nicko and Tim's mothers approached me individually. Fortunately, I found them to be considerate and supportive. Their sons had shared the content of our meeting with their families. Since the parents had known about the sexual explorations before our meeting, they weren't in shock. What they were mostly worried about, was the seriousness of Pasong's actions, and the fate of this boy. They wanted to know what could be done for him? Who to contact?

I did not want the parents in our class to get personally involved. The matter belonged to Pasong's family. It was not easy to reassure them while preserving Pasong's confidentiality. I told them that I was working closely with Pasong's family, and that we were doing everything in our power to give him the help and support he needed. I added that I continued to be committed to keeping all of my students safe at school.

One morning two weeks later, as Pasong's mother was dropping him off at school, she asked to speak with me. I immediately noticed something was wrong. An elegant professional who usually dressed in stylish clothes, Karen didn't look like herself that morning. She wore baggy sweat pants and running shoes. Her eyes were puffy and red, her long curly hair disheveled. She explained that the previous night right after his therapy session with Hank, Pasong had spent time alone with George, his dad. He told him that while in Bangkok, in the homeless street life he had led, in a random encounter, he had been raped.

The brutality of Karen's words sank in as we stood together in a quiet recess of our school hallway, silent tears rolling down our faces.

"I wish I could have protected him from getting hurt," said Karen. "I can't believe he's been living with this horrible memory, and never said a word to us about it for the last two years."

"Karen, it's not like he was hiding it from you. He couldn't talk about it earlier, because he just didn't have the words to say it."

Winning Is Everything

As we approached the end of the school year, the children were in for a great surprise. Only three problems had been written up in the class notebook the preceding week! Everyone in the room was jubilant. In fact, when I announced the good news, the children jumped up and clapped.

"Children....Children...," I tried to speak, but my voice was drowned among the congratulatory cheers. I didn't want to deny the children their moment of glory, so I waited a bit. Then, when things calmed down, I asked, "Does anyone care to comment?"

Many hands went up. The children were proud of our class; they were surprised, relieved. Questions popped up, too, "Mona, do you remember when we used to have twenty problems a week?" and "Will we still have class meetings even if we don't have problems in the notebook?"

"Yes, I remember when we used to have twenty problems a week," I said in a monotonic voice, my head and shoulders drooping. Then I added, "I'll let you in on a secret. On those days I was so frustrated I wanted to call in sick and skip doing the meetings."

My candidness elicited sympathy from some children, and shock from others. I didn't mind their indignation. It was important for them to know that class meetings were not only hard for them, but also for me. Of course, now that we were in a celebratory mood, we could afford reminiscing our earlier hardships. We had gained enough distance, and were victorious, after all.

"And let me answer your other question. Yes, we will continue to have class meetings even if the notebook is blank, because even if on a given week you don't have any problems, I might want to discuss some issues with you. And if there's nothing to discuss, then it'll be your Free Choice time."

"Children, I'm curious. I'd like to know why you think we're having fewer problems now?"

"We can solve our problems on our own. It's like we don't need to write every little problem we have."

"I don't know, but maybe the contracts helped."

"I think we're a nicer community now."

"Class meetings helped us. I mean, we talk about the things that are hard for us, and that makes us care about each other."

"Maybe it's because it's almost the end of the school year, and now we've kinda learned new ways to get along."

"Maybe we...like...listen better to each other."

"I am proud of you," I said, feeling all choked up. "Look at how much you've grown! Look at all the things we've learned about one another!"

The children were touched by my words, maybe a little embarrassed by the intensity of my feelings. I'm not a teacher who lavishes a lot of praise on my students, so when I say I'm proud of them, it carries authenticity and weight.

"All right," I said as I looked down at the class notebook, "We've still got some work to do, and we're going to do a terrific job. I know we will."

Out of the three problems in the notebook, I chose to read the one that had the broadest appeal. It had to do with sportsmanship.

> "On the lawn we played soccer. Pasong was using bad sportsmanship and bad language to players. He just wants to win. We don't care if we win or we lose. We just want to play."
>
> — Joseph, Leo, Tim, Jeremiah, and William

All year we had skirted around the issue of sportsmanship. Not that we'd never mentioned it before. In fact, at the beginning of the year we had talked about being a "good sport", about doing your best and having fun. Yet, we'd never devoted a whole meeting to sportsmanship. As I read the above journal entry, I wondered why it was hard for some children to lose, while others seemed to manage well with defeat, and what could be done to improve the situation? I didn't see this entry as another "Pasong problem," but as an issue from which everyone could benefit.

"Joseph, the entry is in your handwriting. Why don't you first tell us about this problem, then your friends can add their perspectives?"

"Okay," Joseph nodded. "Yesterday at hockey, Pasong kept saying kind of mean things every time the other team scored a goal. It made me mad, 'cause it wasn't fun to play anymore." His face turned into a great big pout.

Everyone looked in Pasong's direction. He sat quietly with no expression. Some children raised their eyebrows as though to say, "Oh, boy, here we go again!"

"Thank you, Joseph. Leo, Jeremiah, William, Tim, do you have anything else you'd like to add?"

"It's kind of like what Joseph said," started Leo. "Pasong shouts at us if we don't pass the puck to him, or if we miss the goal. I don't want to play with him anymore." Leo who was usually tentative, seemed resolute today. Perhaps the solidarity of his buddies gave him strength.

"Thanks, Leo. Anyone else?"

Jeremiah, William and Tim shook their heads.

"Pasong, your turn," I said as I gestured to him.

"I have a hard time losing," he said in a straightforward voice. Not whiny, not defensive, just calm.

I sat still for a moment. After a year of class meetings, Pasong was beginning to take responsibility for his actions, and talk openly without making excuses. In addition, he'd stopped saying he didn't know why he had done something, or didn't remember that it had happened.

"Saying this takes a lot of courage," I said. "Many people aren't even aware they have a hard time losing, and those who know it about themselves, are usually embarrassed to admit it, even grown-ups."

Pasong was trying to contain the pride bursting inside him. A grin stretched itself across his face. His contract had helped him make such progress that I didn't want to dwell on this incident and single him out again as the problem student in our class. He didn't need to feel defeated and discouraged right now.

"You know, children, one person in our class used to have a hard time when we played sports, and recently I've noticed that he's handling things so much better."

I paused, and looked around the room. The class was enjoying the mystery. Faces were scrutinizing other faces, and then I saw him playing with the fringes of a blanket. He grinned at me with recognition.

"William, you guessed I was talking about you, right?" He nodded, his page-boy bangs bouncing on his forehead. "Tell us how you've changed."

William's initial response was hesitant. Perhaps my question was too broad, or too complex for an eight-year-old. It is often difficult for most children to see themselves changing, or to comment about their change.

"I don't know," he started, fumbling for words. "But I remember I used to win at soccer all the time when I was a little kid. Then when I joined my soccer team, I began losing a lot of games. Then I started to win again."

Where is this going, William? I thought to myself. Giving the children a chance to talk was always a risky business. I never knew what was coming.

He continued, "It's like I say to myself, 'Next time you'll try to win.'" He shrugged his shoulders and added, "I don't know, but it works."

"It's hard to explain things that are happening inside us. Isn't it? We sometimes don't have the right words, especially if we're still in the middle of changing. But William, I think I understand what you're saying. Correct me if I'm wrong. You're saying that as you're growing up you're realizing that sometimes we win, and sometimes we lose. That means you're becoming flexible. And when you lose, you don't give up, but instead you hope to win next time."

He smiled, pleased with my interpretation.

"Let me ask all of you, children, and please, be as honest as you can. Who feels really bad when losing at sports or at games, not just a little bit bad, but really bad?"

Only one hand went up. Pasong's. He didn't drop it immediately when realizing that he was the only one. I was sure there were others who didn't raise their hands, others who didn't have Pasong's courage, or self-awareness. But that was all right.

"Thank you." I chose not to make a comment. "Now who could not accept losing last year, but feels better able to tolerate losing this year?"

Sofia, Nina, Erin, and William raised their hands. This last question had elicited more responses. More honesty.

"I have an idea that might help Pasong say, 'Next time I'll try to win'. Pasong, next week when we play sports, what if you and William play on the same team? This way, if your team loses, maybe William's attitude about losing can help you imagine that there is a next time, and that maybe that next time is a winning time. What do you say, guys?"

Pasong and William were euphoric! I usually didn't put them together, because they were strong players, and I needed to balance the teams. But I knew I could find a way to manage evening things out.

"Let's try to see if this will help."

Jeremiah had been raising his hand for a while.

"Jeremiah, we don't have much time, but go ahead, make it snappy."

In a single breath he blurted out, "I just want to say that I like it when my teammates say something nice to me when I miss a goal, something like 'Nice try'."

"Thank you for saying that. Children, do you think people on your team would take risks if they were teased or put down every time they missed a move?" I didn't wait for their answer. "Of course, not! They'd feel worse, 'cause it's harder to try when people don't trust your ideas, and don't forgive you for making mistakes. So let's try this week to support one another, and roll with the punches."

• • •

The last three weeks of school proved to be almost free from conflicts in the playground. The children played games cooperatively. Placing Pasong and William together on the same team helped improve Pasong's attitude, but only to a limited extent. Tolerating defeat was not easy for him. Winning at sports was everything to him, almost a way of staying alive.

One day near the end of the school year as I was supervising lunch, an impromptu, child-generated game of soccer was underway on the sports field. From a distance I could see Pasong, Nicko, Tim, Robbie, William, Jeremiah, Ben, Joseph—the usual cast of characters.

I chatted with one of the other lunch duty teachers, when suddenly I heard a loud cheer coming from the sports field. I turned my head, and saw Nicko and William jumping up and down, slapping palms, and screaming with joy. I inched myself a little closer where I could see Pasong crouched on the grass, his fine hair dripping wet, his hands covering his face.

"It's okay, Pasong. It's only one goal," said Joseph who was leaning down next to him, patting him on the back.

"No, it's not," hissed Pasong as he uncovered his face, and stood up. "Jeremiah sucks! He can't block a goal! I'm gonna tell him he can't be on my team!"

But Joseph ran after Pasong, pulling his t-shirt. "No! No! Pasong" he pleaded. "Remember your contract! You don't wanna miss sports again! We need you on our team."

Pasong stopped, and with a loud grunt his hot face got all scrunched up into a grimace, and the tears rolled down his cheeks as though he were squeezing them out of his eyes. He made a fist with one hand, and slammed it hard into the palm of his other hand.

CHAPTER TWO

The Class as a Community

Molly, A Child in Crisis

Over the years I've seen how a crisis at home can affect a child at school, and have repercussions on the other students in the classroom. Losing a pet, the separation of parents, the illness or death of a family member, all can affect how well a child can cope at school.

It was ironic that around Halloween, just when my students' excitement was barely containable, was also when Molly's mother, June, was diagnosed with breast cancer. A nasty case.

After school, as I was taking down the construction-paper pentominoes from our math bulletin board, Vince, my principal, came up the stairs to tell me the news. "Breast Cancer." There is nothing more terrifying to women than the sound of those two words. I quickly thought back at how a few weeks ago at our class fall picnic June had looked so young and healthy in her long pink dress and straw hat.

Vince, who last year had lost his own mother to cancer after a protracted battle, was acutely aware of the needs of a family in crisis. We talked about ways to help Molly deal with her feelings in the classroom, and how the school might be of support to the entire family. Then Vince went back to his office, while I sat staring into space. I cried, of course, for June and for Molly.

The next day, as the children hung their coats and backpacks on the hooks outside my door, and stepped inside the classroom, I realized they needed a class meeting as soon as possible. Many of them had heard that something was wrong with Molly's mom, and were now nervously talking and looking around.

Then I saw Molly with her father, John, standing by the door. She was leaning against his shoulder, her eyes cast down—a tall, slender child with a long neck, and the straight back of a ballerina. Her ears stuck out a little, and her eyes were bright blue like forget-me-nots. Molly's strawberry-blond hair was always neatly pulled back, sometimes in a bun, sometimes in a pony tail. Today it was in a French braid, making her look older.

I told John and Molly how sorry I was to hear that June was ill, and asked Molly whether she'd like to tell the class about her mother. "You tell them," she whispered.

After everyone settled on the rug, I took a deep breath, and said, "Children, we're having an emergency class meeting this morning, because there's something I need to tell you." Then I looked at Molly to give her another chance to talk if she happened to have changed her mind. But she slowly shook her head.

"Children, Molly would like me to tell you that her mother is sick. Her mom has breast cancer."

Molly, who was sitting next to me, nudged herself a little closer.

Then Rachel said, "I already knew, 'cause, see, last night Molly's mom called my mom on the phone." And with a quick motion of her fingers, she pointed back and forth from Molly to herself, and added, "And then we talked."

Molly nodded, a faint smile on her lips. We all knew Rachel and Molly were best friends.

Nina raised her hand. "You know, last year my Auntie Doris had cancer, too, but now she's all better." Then looking at Molly, she added, "I'm sorry about your mom."

Ben told us about his Grandpa George's heart attack. Jack described the day his neighbor slipped in the driveway and broke her leg. And then Sofia said in a tentative voice, "Sometimes I worry about my dad. See, he's got...uh." She hesitated. "I don't know what it's called...uh...well, anyway, he has to give himself a shot every day." A few children made faces and groaning sounds.

For a few minutes, I was letting the children take the lead with the content of our meeting. Even though it was good for Molly to hear that other children have had to deal with the illness and accidents of their loved ones, I didn't want us to dwell too long on the tragedies of life. Molly didn't need to carry everybody's burden today.

Nina had expressed empathy toward Molly, and others had identified with the unspoken anxiety around accidents and illness. However, no one had asked Molly specific questions. In fact, very few children talked to her directly. I gathered that at this moment Molly's news was disturbing to them, and the only thing they knew how to do, was to relate her experience to their own lives.

We spent a little while longer on the rug, and before getting up, I said, "You know, children, it was good to talk this morning. Thank you for telling us your stories. How can we help Molly right now?"

"We could play with her."

"Or invite her to sit at lunch with us."

"I like to make cards, so I'll draw her a picture of a horse, 'cause I know she likes horses."

"I don't know if Molly would like someone to sit on a bench with her at recess, but sometimes I kinda like it when my friends do that."

At recess I followed my brood to the playground. Molly was, of course, playing with Rachel. I sat on a nearby bench, and watched them on the basketball court, running like two young foals with lanky legs and flying manes. Under the hoop with a rubber ball between her hands, Molly's life seemed unchanged.

Perhaps it was Rachel's boisterous nature that helped Molly stay afloat. Rachel was skinny and wiry, with long, wavy unruly brown hair which she tried unsuccessfully to tame with clips and gel. She was active, funny, and forever rushing. Very different from Molly who was slow and elegant, almost deliberate in her movements. Yet these two girls with contrasting faces and tempos were inseparable.

Fortunately life provides us with small distractions. Molly was excited about trick-or-treating with Rachel, and the slumber party that would follow at Rachel's house, but most of all, she was consumed by her costume. She was going to be a waitress from the fifties, and was full of ideas about her uniform, the tray she was going to carry, the Coke bottle and plastic fries, and, especially, the way she was going to do her hair.

But after Halloween had come and gone, after Molly had been flooded with the initial outpouring of affection, the visitors who stopped by to bring flowers or dinner in a basket, when life returned to its regular routine, she realized that something was very wrong. June was forever gone, consulting with different physicians about the best course of treatment, busy on the phone with friends or relatives. Molly didn't have the words for what was happening. The only thing she knew was that she missed her mommy.

The first clue I observed of the effects of June's illness on her daughter, was that during read-aloud chapter book on the rug, Molly would lean into me as though she were an appendage of mine, like an extra arm, connected to my side, an extension of my body. Then over the steady drone of my voice, I would hear a slow slurping sound. Molly would be sucking her thumb.

Then a few days later Molly came to school with Ringo, her stuffed raccoon. He had the most wonderful little mask on his face, and a giant striped bushytail.

Molly's face exploded with joy as she introduced him to me in a resounding theatrical voice, "Mona, this is Ringo the Magnificent, with rings on his tail!" Then instantly her face clouded over. "Is it okay I brang him to school?"

"Well, of course, Molly," I quickly reassured her. Then turning to Ringo I said, "I'm glad to meet you Ringo, the Magnificent. Perhaps you could come over to my backyard and talk to the raccoons who raid our trash cans every night!"

Molly's eyes widened as she caught on to my joke. "Yeah, he could probably do it. He can do anything!"

And that's how Ringo became a regular member of our class. None of the other children questioned his presence, or imitated Molly by bringing their own stuffed animals to school. It's as though everyone understood that Molly needed Ringo. Most of the day he sat on top of the cubby cabinet, but when she needed him, he was on her lap.

June and her doctors decided that a radical mastectomy would improve her prognosis. Molly came to school carrying Ringo tightly in her arms.

"My mom's gonna have surgery."

"I know, sweetie," I said as I enveloped her and Ringo in a big embrace.

We were quiet for a moment. Then she said, "You know what the good part is?"

"No," I said unbelieving that there could be a good part in this story.

"My grandma's coming to stay with us."

I gathered from Molly's enthusiasm that Grandma would have to be a pretty special lady. And she was.

A week later I met Grandma Edna. She marched into my classroom, and with an unparalleled New England accent proceeded to introduce herself.

"I'm Edna McCormick, Molly's grandmother. You must be Mona."

I felt immediately in awe of this tall, energetic woman with short gray hair and metal-rimmed glasses. There was something about her stature, her posture, or her strong handshake that told me right away that she was a no-nonsense woman. It turned out she had been a high school principal in Providence, Rhode Island. Her weathered face was full of kindness and wisdom, while her eyebrows, dark and thick, made her look younger than her age. Her eyes were blue, like Molly's.

"I'm here to take charge of the family," she said briskly.

Every day Grandma drove the station wagon to school. In the morning I would sometimes see their car stop under my window. Molly, her big sister, Stephanie, and little Vanessa would tumble out of the car as Grandma kissed every cheek, and made sure each girl had her lunch bag and back pack.

One day after June had come home from the hospital, Molly approached me at recess, and sat down next to me on the bench.

"My mom's gonna start her treatment today. I can't get to be with her, 'cause she can get sick if she catches my germs," she said, her blue eyes dimmed of their brilliant color.

"I'm sorry, Molly. This must be very hard for you."

I wrapped an arm around her shoulders, and she surprised me by snuggling her face in my chest.

"Today is Friday, perhaps you can write about your feelings in our class notebook, and everyone can help you at class meeting," I said gently.

"No, I don't want to write in the class notebook."

I knew how private she was, yet I also knew she needed to talk about her mother. "You know, Molly, when something important happens to one person in our class, it's good to share it with the group. If you don't want to write it yourself, would you mind if I write something for you? Would that be all right?"

She thought for a moment, then she said with no affect whatsoever, "I guess it's okay."

So I wrote my entry, and later that day at our meeting I read it to the class. I addressed the class by the name the children had chosen for themselves that year—Slippery Lizards.

Dear Slippery Lizards,
Molly asked me if she could talk to the class about something that's happening in her family.

Love, Mona

Everyone was serious in anticipation of the news.

"Molly, tell us some more about it."

She spoke in a slow manner, stretching her words, as though talking was an immeasurable effort. "I can't be with my mom." She played nervously with a strand of her hair. "She's going to the hospital again, and the doctor is giving her some medicine to kill the cancer, but now she can catch all kinds of germs."

"Molly, can you talk to her on the telephone?" I asked.

"I don't know. I think my dad said Mommy's sleeping a lot."

"It's hard when someone you love is sick," I said.

A few children talked about grandparents who had been ill or who had died, parents who were in accidents, or hospitalized. And William told us about the day his cat Mittens got hit by a car.

"Children, many of you have shared difficult things that have happened to your loved ones. Now let me ask you something. What's the hardest thing for you when someone you love is ill?"

Without hesitation, Kate blurted out, "Not being able to see them. One time my Dad had to have surgery, and kids weren't allowed in his room. I hated that rule."

"I hate it when my mom's on a business trip and I can't talk to her," said Nina.

Jeremiah was eager to talk, and as usually was squirming on the rug.

"Yes, Jeremiah, what's the hardest thing for you when someone you love is sick?"

"When my grandma had a heart attack, I worried a lot, like I couldn't go to sleep at night, 'cause I didn't know if she was gonna get better or if she was gonna die."

"Did she die?" asked Nicko.

"No, she got better, but she's real weak now. She used to bake me the best chocolate chip cookies, but she gets tired real quick now."

Molly recognized herself in Jeremiah's words, and added, "Yeah, that's what happened to me last night. I couldn't sleep so Grandma had to stay in my room with me for a while."

"I get nightmares," said Joseph in a whisper.

"When my mom is sick, I get...hum...cranky," said Rosie. "My daddy calls me 'Little Miss Cranky.'"

I appreciated the comic relief.

"Children, let's shift our thoughts to the things that might help us when we're worried or lonesome. Molly told us that last night having her grandma stay by her bedside helped her. What else helps you?"

"I like it when people ask me to play with them," said Heather.

"I like to write or draw in my diary," said Sofia.

"Playing basketball is the best for me. It makes me forget everything," said Pasong.

"Maybe we could all make cards for Molly and her mom," said Nina.

"That's a great idea!" I exclaimed.

For some children talking about how to comfort themselves had been easy; others looked blankly at me as though I had been speaking in a foreign language. How could they have known how they felt in times of duress, if no one had ever asked them to reflect on what it was they needed?

"Molly, what would you like from us? Would you like company in the playground at recess and lunch, or do you need time by yourself?" I asked.

"I like it if people ask me to play."

"Good, now we know what you need. However, if some days you feel you need time by yourself, just let us know. At home I let my kids know if I need my privacy. Sometimes I like having my cat on my lap rather than talking to people."

Just as I was about to wrap things up, Pasong wanted to say something.

"I wish I had the power to live as long as I wanted. I feel scared about when it's my time to go," he said.

"You know, Pasong, I used to feel just like you, but one day I asked my neighbor, Lorna who is eighty-seven years old if she was afraid to die. She said no. She said she was ready to die."

Pasong interrupted me, "I guess when you're that old you're ready to die."

"Yes, and you're still young, Pasong, you have a whole life ahead of you."

In talking about his fear of dying, Pasong had zeroed in on my unspoken anxiety. I wondered if Molly had wanted to tell us she was worried her mom might die. June's possible death had stood unrecognized amidst us like the elephant in the room everyone sees, but doesn't mention.

• • •

One early morning the following week, Edna was at my classroom door, alone, while the children were playing outside in the playground.

She stood tall and stiff like a cardboard paper doll. "How's Molly doing?" she asked.

"Pretty well considering all the changes she's having to adjust to," I said. "Last week when June started chemotherapy, Molly was miserable not to be able to see her or talk to her. We had a class meeting, and the children offered their support and friendship."

"Oh, I'm grateful you're discussing everything so openly at school. At home Molly tends to hold things inside. But recently she's been complaining about not wanting to come to school. She wants to stay home. Has she told you anything?"

"No, she hasn't. But Mrs. McCormick..."

"Please call me Edna."

"Edna, I understand that Molly might want to be with you and June, but I don't think it's a good idea for her to be away from her friends, her world, and the regularity of her days at school. Don't you think so?" I asked as though I were talking to a colleague.

"To be honest with you, I don't know. I've been out of the classroom for so many years, I don't know what is best for Molly. It's too close to home. I can't think straight." She shook her head in desperation.

"Edna, from all that I've read about children in crisis, I know they need regular routines. I also know we need to maintain the same expectations from them. John and June expect Molly to be at school. That's her job. June's job is to get better; yours is to take care of the family. We have to help Molly remain at school."

"All right. But it just breaks my heart to see that young one so distraught about her mama," said Edna.

"How are Stephanie and Vanessa doing?" I asked.

"Oh, well, Stephanie is very involved with her ballet classes, and her social life. You know how it is with twelve-year-olds. And Vanessa is too young to comprehend what's going on. It's Molly who's the most affected right now. She's always been the family blotting paper!"

"Let's work on this together, Edna," I said. "I don't want to make it harder on Molly or on you."

She started to walk out the door, then stopped and turned back to me to say, "Don't you worry about me, dear. I come from hardy stock. The McCormicks are survivors."

The next morning Molly was crouched by the coat hooks. She was whimpering and pleading with her grandmother.

"But Grandma, I want to go home, and stay with you and Mommy!"

I approached them. "Molly," I said softly as I bent down to face her. "The kids and I want you to stay at school with us. There are so many wonderful things scheduled for today. You don't want to miss working on our story plays, do you?"

Molly's whimpering turned into loud sobs and cries. She didn't want to hear me.

Edna talked to her kindly, but firmly. "Molly, you can't stay with me and Mommy today. I have to take her to the doctor for her appointment."

"But, Grandma, I want to come with you."

"Molly, Molly," I tried to reason with her, "You'll have more fun at school than in the doctor's waiting-room, and before you know it, Grandma'll be here to pick you up."

"But what if...what if...," she hiccuped and choked. "What if she doesn't come back?" She looked at me with her piercing blue eyes that beckoned me to be honest.

"She'll be here, you'll see. Right, Grandma?" I turned to Edna who was standing by my side, looking helpless and on the verge of crying. She didn't look as tall or as strong anymore. Molly's tearful scene had worn her down.

"Yes, Pumpkin, I'll be here. I'll pick you, Stephanie and Vanessa up by the gate, as usual. Please, don't worry."

I asked Edna to say good-bye to Molly and leave immediately. Prolonged good-byes made things worse. A quick exit down the stairs was preferable.

In a frenzy Molly held on to her grandmother's raincoat and pulled with the claws of a furious kitten. After hugging Molly, Edna quickly disengaged herself, and ran down the stairs without looking back. But at the bottom of the stairwell she looked up, and saw me holding a broken-down Molly in my arms.

By now all my students as well as the students from the classroom across the hall were alarmed by Molly's display of tears. Everyone was in the hallway, talking, and hovering around us.

"Is Molly okay?" they asked.

I became overwhelmed by the commotion and chaos around me. Rachel ran inside the classroom and brought us a box of tissues. Molly wiped her face while I tried to calm her down before walking her into the classroom.

When we finally stepped over the threshold of my doorway, I thought Molly was going to be all right. Wrong. Molly flopped herself down at one of the small individual tables on the periphery of the classroom. Rachel came over and sat down at a nearby table, her face pale and tense. She patted Molly on the back.

I shut the door behind me and stood in front of my class. I needed to say something to my students who sat looking at me with mournful and expectant eyes.

"Children, Molly's very unhappy this morning. She didn't want to leave her grandma."

To normalize things for Molly and the others, and perhaps a little bit for myself, too, I added, "It happens to all of us once in a while."

"Yeah," said Erin, "sometimes I cry when my mom leaves me with a baby-sitter."

Molly started crying softly again. How was I going to teach my class today when Molly was so upset? And how could I take care of Molly's needs with all the other demands placed on me as a teacher?

"Molly, do you think you could sit at your table and copy down your spelling list with the rest of the class?" I asked gently to help distract her.

She nodded and moved over to her table. However, she didn't pick up her pencil and write down her words. Instead, she covered her face with her hands. Every few minutes we could hear her muffled cries under a wad of crumpled tissues.

Sofia brought Molly extra tissues; Kate, Nina and Rachel came by and patted her back. We were all worried and upset. I wanted to hold her in my arms and rock her gently, yet I was acutely aware I'd be crossing a barrier. How can a teacher be comforting while maintaining the proper boundaries with her students?

Molly cried on and off most of the morning. Her classmates and I consoled her when we could, and there were times when she wanted to retreat to the pillows in the book corner and be by herself. At lunch time she asked to call her grandmother.

"Grandma, when are you coming to pick me up?" she asked between sobs. "Okay....I love you, too, Grandma....Okay, here's Mona."

When Molly left the staff room, I spoke briefly with Edna.

"She's been crying all morning, Edna. I'm not sure I did the right thing."

"But what else can we do? I couldn't have taken her with me to the doctor. A little girl should not be spending her morning in an oncologist's office," she said.

"Edna, let me talk to Vince, I'll get back to you."

A few minutes after hanging up the telephone, I was standing in Vince's office lamenting to him about my mistake.

"I shouldn't have insisted she stay at school. How could my instincts have been so wrong? She's inconsolable, Vince. Nothing I say or do seems to help. I've never seen a child so upset for such an extend period of time. It's like a break-down of some sort."

Vince tried to reassure me. "You acted with Molly's best interests in mind. You expected her to move on from the initial tears at the door of the classroom, and get engaged in the curriculum and with her friends. Most children can do that."

"Vince, what's even worse, is that the rest of the children are becoming undone. They're so upset, I can't tell you. Some of them are so preoccupied by Molly's suffering that they can't seem to focus on their work. They knew her as a leader, a sturdy member of the class, and now she's falling apart."

Vince suggested that Molly spend some time with him in his office. He, too, was worried about the effects of Molly's tears on the rest of the class.

In the afternoon when the children got paired off for Partner Reading, I saw Molly crawling over to our book corner, and curling up into a ball under the table.

"Molly, Heather is waiting for you for Partner Reading," I said.

"I can't...I can't," she said between sobs.

"Molly," I said softly as I crawled to join her under the table. "Is it too hard to do anything right now?" I wrapped my arms around her.

She nodded, her small chest heaving.

"Listen, I spoke to Vince about how hard the morning has been for you, and he suggested you go visit him for a bit. How would that be for you?"

She removed a mountain of soaking tissues from her red and puffy eyes, and looked up at me.

"I don't know," she mumbled.

Like most children at our school, Molly was fond of Vince and intrigued by his collection of magic tricks which he kept on his desk. Children were seldom sent to his office to be punished. On the contrary, they were often sent there when they needed some tender loving care. Every child who spent some time in Vince's office came back cheered up and eager to show off a new magic trick.

Encouraged by my talk, Molly spent a part of the afternoon with Vince while I focused on my class. When she came back, I expected her to make a quarter appear from behind my ear, or pull a flower from her pocket. But no, she came back quiet and somber and dragging her feet. She sat down at her table with eyes that were miles away from our classroom.

"What time is it?" she asked Rachel who was sitting next to her. She was counting the minutes to go home.

When Edna came to pick up Molly and her sisters, I had a brief private moment to talk with her.

"Edna, it was hard for Molly to be away from you today. Her distress was too severe. I can't imagine her, me or the kids going through something like that again tomorrow. It's too much pain for a child to have to bear. She's worried about her mom, and because she's come to rely on you now, she's afraid to lose you, too."

Edna listened to me and nodded. "Of course you're right, but what can I do?"

"In talking with Vince I've decided that since Molly can't stay home with June, would you be able to stay at school with her for a few days?"

Edna agreed to try it for a few days, and then see if Molly could find the strength to be at school on her own. Edna also agreed to call the family psychotherapist, and ask if he could see Molly as soon as possible.

That evening at home I misplaced my wallet. I looked for it for a few minutes, and then frustrated and defeated, I broke down and cried. My family didn't understand what was happening to me. I didn't understand it either. I blamed it on my hormones (something I've been doing more readily at this particular juncture in my life). My youngest son eventually found the wallet between the pillows of the couch. But I went to bed feeling annoyed at my tearful evening.

It was only the next morning, when two parents approached me to tell me that their children had been fragile and teary the evening before, that I realized how deeply we had all been affected by Molly's pain. If she was afraid of separating from her mother and grandmother, maybe she had a valid point. Perhaps the children, like me, were becoming worried about losing our loved ones, too.

Edna remained in our classroom for a week. She sat in the back of the room at a little desk. I explained to the class that Molly needed her grandmother nearby, and everyone seemed to understand. Molly sat with her classmates, and would occasionally turn around to glance at Grandma and make sure she was really there. Grandma would flash her a great big smile, and that would suffice. Molly could then resume her work.

On Friday morning I was getting ready for our class meeting. I had written an entry about Molly's distress this week. I wanted us to talk about it as a class with Molly. However, when Molly and Edna arrived, they announced that they were leaving before lunch because June had a medical appointment in the afternoon. Edna had wanted Molly to remain at school, but Molly didn't want anything to do with her grandmother's idea. I decided not to insist.

So Molly left at noon, and after lunch we gathered on the rug to have our class meeting. I read my entry, even though Molly wasn't with us, because the children and I needed to talk about the stresses of our week.

Dear Slippery Lizards,

This week we were all very aware of how sad Molly has been in our class. You've all been great to her. How can we continue to support her? And how does it feel for you when you have to separate from your parents? Did any of you experience the same worries as Molly?

Let's talk,

Love, Mona

We went around the room telling our separation stories and worries about losing our parents. There was an urgency in their voices.

"I remember I cried the first day of kindergarten," said Shireen who usually sat quietly and watched. "The teacher holded me when my mom had to leave the room, and I started to kick and scream." She smiled with a surprised look on her face as if to say, "I can't believe I used to be this kid."

"I cried when I had to take my first swimming lesson," said Joseph. "I wanted my mom to get into the pool with me; I didn't want to go with the teacher."

"When I was in preschool, nobody played with me," said Kate who was getting tearful. "My hair used to be really short," she said as she motioned to her earlobes. "And the kids used to say I was a boy."

"You know," I said, "I still remember how upset I had felt when my parents went away on a trip, and left me and my little sister with our nanny. I must have been six years old, it's been ages ago, but I still remember how angry and abandoned I had felt."

"I worry when my mom is late coming to pick me up from Karate," said Jack.

"One time I had to wait in *After School*, and I was the last one to get picked up. I thought my mom forgot me, or something," said Nicko.

"That must have been hard for you," I said. "This week has been very hard for Molly. It wasn't easy for us, either."

"Yeah," said Nina, "she wasn't like usual, you know, funny and stuff."

"I miss playing with her," said Rachel quietly.

"Can you guess why Molly's having such a hard time separating from her grandma?" I asked.

"'Cause she wants to stay home with her mom and her grandma," said Ben.

"I think it's 'cause she's scared something bad's gonna happen to her mom," said Rachel.

"Is that what you think, or something she told you," I asked.

"No, she didn't say anything, but last night my mom and I talked about Molly."

"Did it help you?"

"Yeah, 'cause see, I was, like, scared my mom would get sick like Molly's mom, but my mom told me not to worry, 'cause she's healthy."

A long silence followed. Rachel had uttered what I had suspected was bothering many of my students—the fear of losing one's mother.

Reading fairy tales to my students about orphans, abandoned kids, cruel stepmothers, and monstrous creatures didn't scare me. I was convinced that fairy tales helped children work through some of their anxieties. However, talking about Molly's fears of losing her mother was too close, too real.

Then Jack asked in a tentative voice, "Can I catch it? I mean, can I get cancer?"

I explained that cancer wasn't contagious like a cold, and that we didn't know why some people got it, while others didn't. And because I so wanted to make them feel better, I added that scientists all over the world were trying to find cures for cancer and other diseases. I had to say something optimistic.

"Mona, how do you feel about Molly's mom being sick?" asked Rachel.

Rachel was able to step away from her own preoccupation in order to attend to the grief of others around her. My first thought was, "Oh, no, how dare one of them get so personal with me?" Then I thought about how honest and courageous they had been to express their most terrifying fears. Was I a coward or was I trying to protect them?

"It always scares me to hear about a mother who has cancer, because I'm a mother, too, and I want to stay as healthy as I can for my children."

I didn't tell them about my friend, Judy who battled for eight years, but finally succumbed to breast cancer.

"I hope Molly's mom gets better soon," said Rachel.

"I hope so, too, Sweetie."

"What if we make her a get-well book?" Nina proposed.

The mood in the room suddenly changed. From feeling defeated and depressed, we became excited at the thought of making a gift for June.

Over the weekend Molly's therapist, Ingrid, called me to check in and see how she was doing. I told her about Edna's presence in the classroom. She agreed that Molly needed her grandmother's support right now. She told me Molly was having nightmares, and had spoken about her dread of losing her mother.

Ingrid was worried that Molly was protecting her mother. Like the dutiful daughter she was, she was feeling responsible and wanted to do the right thing. She had even told her she didn't want to upset her mom and cry in front of her.

"What can I do to help?" I asked.

"Remain the same for Molly. Don't get stricter than you were before June got sick, don't indulge her. Be the same predictable teacher she knows."

On Monday when Edna came up to my classroom with a clingy Molly in tow, I understood that spending the weekend with her family was making it harder for Molly to separate from Edna.

I remembered Ingrid's words, and it occurred to me to present Molly with a contract to help her with some limits. It wasn't good for her to feel so out of control.

"Molly, let's sit down, you, me and Grandma. We need to talk."

Luckily my class went off to music, so the three of us could have a private meeting. I placed a piece of paper on the table and printed: MOLLY'S CONTRACT.

"We're going to make a deal. You promise to do your job of coming to school every day, and Grandma will promise to do her job of picking you up."

"But I don't want Grandma to leave me," Molly resisted.

"Grandma's job is to help the whole family," I said firmly. To soften the blow, I added, "She didn't come all the way from Providence to spend her days pretending to be a third-grader!"

"I already know my multiplication tables!" Edna pointed out with a smile. Molly had to smile, too.

"Then I'll stay at home with her and Mommy," said Molly. I was delighted to see her feistiness reemerge.

"No, Molly, your job is to come to school," I repeated. "And that's why we're going to draft this contract together. It's going to help you be able to let go of Grandma a little at a time. Look..."

I started to write as I spoke:

"Molly's part: Molly will stay at school all day as usual. She will do her school work and be strong and brave until Grandma comes to pick her up.

Mona's part: Mona will teach third grade as usual, and will be available to listen during recess and lunch if Molly wants to talk.

Grandma's part: Grandma will stay at school in the morning for a little while to help Molly get settled, then she will leave to do her jobs. Every day she will stay less and less time at school. In the afternoon she will pick up Molly as usual.

Grandma's schedule: The first day Grandma will stay till lunch."

I stopped writing, and looked up at Molly. She was quietly absorbed by what I was doing.

"Molly, how long do you think Grandma should stay the second day?" I asked casually.

"I...I...don't know. Maybe till 11:30," she offered.

"Okay," I said as I jotted down 11:30. "What about the third day and the fourth? We need to make up the contract for the whole week."

Molly proposed 11:00 for the third day, 10:30 for the fourth, and 10:00 for Friday the last day.

"All right, then," I said. "Next week we'll make up a new contract cutting Grandma's time at school shorter and shorter. Now let's all three of us sign our names and date this contract."

To make our deal more official, I put out my hand, and shook hands with Molly and Grandma. Everyone seemed pleased. But this was the easy part of the deal. The hard part would come later as Molly would have to extricate herself from Edna's arms.

After the children came back from their music class, we all sat down on the rug together (Edna included). I announced to them that Molly, Grandma and I had signed a contract, and I explained how it worked. It was important that we all support Molly in her attempts at becoming stronger and more independent.

"But what does Molly have to give up if she doesn't do her part?" asked Pasong who was following this discussion very closely.

"Good question, Pasong," I said. "But, you know, this contract is not exactly like your self-governing contract." I had to think fast. Why was this contract different?

And then I understood why. "You see, in this case, when Molly cries and doesn't do her part, she's giving up being a member of our class. Crying and not participating are hard enough, so I don't think she needs to give up anything else. It wouldn't make any sense. Do you know what I mean?" I said looking around at my group. They nodded.

"Yeah, it's like crying is her punishment," said Robbie. Not very tactful, but he made sense to the other children.

Then we moved on to telling Molly about the class meeting she had missed on Friday, and the book we wanted to write for her mother. She was immediately enthusiastic. Because I knew how much children liked fairy tales, I suggested that the get-well book be based on characters from fairy tales who brave terrifying obstacles and emerge victorious.

That same morning the children began to write and draw. Some showed June drinking potions that made her healthy. Other children drew pictures of June, in full armor, battling her cancer with a sharp and shiny sword. Still others portrayed the cancer as a dragon or demon with June taming it until it became as tiny and harmless as a kitten. Tim created a scenario where June built herself a house of brick while the cancer, disguised as the big bad wolf, stood outside huffing and puffing. Heather showed June pushing her cancer, in the form of a nasty old witch, into an oven. Every page of the book seemed to be inspired by a famous fairy tale. Every page contained an image of power and victory over the evil and dangerous disease.

At lunch when Edna said good-bye to Molly, I saw their tight embrace, and I understood how hard this was.

"I wish Grandma could stay the rest of the day," Molly sighed with tears welling up in her eyes.

"I know," is all I could say.

The good-bye scenes of the rest of the week remained difficult for Molly, but she was faithful to her promise. As she began to successfully separate from Edna, her courage and confidence returned. She became more invested in her school life again, writing poems at writers' workshop, building her magnet experiment with her science partners, participating at sports and music, and generally being more active and playful with her friends.

Edna and I did our parts, too. Every day that went by successfully, I would flash a thumbs-up to Edna as she drove out of the school parking lot.

The second week went even more smoothly. Molly was now used to the contract routine. When the last day of the contract arrived, the day Edna was to drop Molly off at the regular school time and depart immediately, Molly ambled easily into the classroom with a group of girls hovering around her like a cloud of bees. Edna who was standing by the classroom door, cleared her throat rather loudly and for obvious comic effect.

"Don't I even get a hug?" she asked teasingly.

"Oh, Grandma, I'm sorry!" exclaimed Molly as she ran back to hug Edna. "Me and Rachel and Nina are planning this story play, and we were talking about our ideas."

• • •

Over the next two weeks we worked hard on June's get-well book, writing, editing, drawing. It helped us all. Molly didn't want to miss a day of school, because she wanted to be a part of this class creation. When the book was finished, I wrote a dedication to June:

To June,
The German poet, Schiller wrote, "Deeper meaning resides in the fairy
tale told to me in my childhood than in the truth that is taught by
life." (The Piccolomini, III, 4.)

You are the bravest and strongest of all heroines!

From Mona and the Slippery Lizards

Even though the book was meant for June, it held its own meaning and healing power for Molly. She loved flipping through the pages and seeing drawings of her mother, strong and clever, outwitting her enemy. Molly drew the cover—a feisty little character, not totally unlike June, wearing a whimsical hat, battling a giant dragon ten times her height. In the corner of the page was June's arsenal of magic potions and weapons. The title in big block letters read, "June, the Conqueror." Finally our class was ready to part with the book and send it with Molly to its rightful owner.

"I wonder if she'll like it," mused Nina.

"She'll love it!" exclaimed Molly wide-eyed and impish-looking.

• • •

The next day Molly arrived at school beaming with joy, carrying an enveloped addressed to me and the Slippery Lizards.

"It's a thank you note from my mom," she said as she helped me unseal it. "Can I read it to the class? Can I, please?"

"Of course. Go right ahead."

Molly's face was radiant as she held her mother's note and read it to the children who had settled all around us on the rug:

Dear Mona and the Slippery Lizards,

Thank you, thank you for your lovely get-well book! I already feel better! Molly and I sat at the kitchen table and read it together. I laughed and I cried. What wonderful writers and artists you are! I will use all of your ideas to get better. Well, almost all of them. I still need to brew a magic concoction, and sharpen my sword!

Yours truly,

June

I reached for a tissue; the children laughed and cheered. Molly folded the note and placed it on my desk.

CHAPTER THREE

Investing Oneself

Jack, The Class Clown

It was 9:00 o'clock. My new class was filing in on the first day of school. Some of the children were wary as they examined the posters on the walls; others were chatting, all excited to be in the big kids' building. It was like the beginning of a party when you're not quite sure whether you'll have a blast of a time, or be bored to death.

"Jack's the class clown," tooted Robbie as he pointed to a freckled-face boy with a shock of red hair.

"And here's the Hoop Champion," Robbie continued as Lamar, walked in, a tall, bony black boy. "And she's the Princess Poet." A small chubby girl in overalls tailed behind the group.

'Oh-uh!' I thought to myself, 'Who's this kid? Who's this Robbie character?'

Every teacher dreads the student who stands out in the first few minutes of the first day of school. It's like an omen of the hardships to come. Yet, Robbie presented himself with such confidence and poise, that a little part of me was intrigued. He wore a red knit polo shirt and light blue jeans. His blond hair was neatly parted to one side, and combed down with gel. A handsome and audacious boy.

After I had gathered the children on the rug for formal introductions, I addressed Robbie's previous informal ones.

"You know, Robbie, I have a hard time with labels. When you called Jack, "Class Clown," Lamar, "Hoop Champion," and Alice, "Princess Poet," there was no room for them to be anything else. Maybe Alice likes scuba diving, too; maybe Lamar listens to rock music; maybe Jack likes gardening.

But the roles you give them make it very limiting for them. People don't like to be categorized for fooling around, or shooting baskets, or writing poems."

I turned to face the rest of the class in the hopes of welcoming everyone into a school year filled with unlimited dreams and opportunities. "What I hope for each and everyone of you this year, is to have more than one role. You can be football players, great actors, stamp collectors, computer whizzes—you can be all of these things and more."

My little speech seemed to have sobered Robbie. And as the weeks wore on his behavior became less brazen, and he settled into the routines of our days.

But it was Jack who became my concern—Jack, with his flaming red locks, his baggy jeans and untied shoelaces. He didn't talk much in class, but he gave the impression of always being on the verge of some shrewdly schemed plot.

Jack's time moved infinitely slowly. It took him longer than anyone else to return to our classroom after recess, lunch, a trip to the bathroom or the water fountain.

"Jack, come on, let's go!" I'd prod as he typically ambled down the halls, admiring every bulletin board in sight, talking to visitors, or stopping to read notes posted on the walls.

When he finally made an appearance in the classroom, he would saunter, his shoulders drooping, his arms dangling alongside his body, his head teetering on his long neck as if it were attached by a precarious string. This boy didn't seem to have a backbone. He resembled those small wooden toys connected with threads, and shaped like animals or cartoon figures that collapse into a heap when you press a button under their feet.

When he'd reach his table, he would plunk himself noisily into his seat, and roll his eyes in an exaggerated manner, eliciting giggles and laughter. Often he'd miss his chair, and tumble down to the floor. At his table he'd sit and survey the rug, looking for pieces of string or scraps of paper. When he found something of interest, he's quickly pick it up, and fiddle with it, his mind elsewhere.

I wasn't sure at first whether he was bored, or couldn't follow what was in progress. Sometimes he'd interrupt my instructions to ask to open a window, or offer to pull down the blinds, or notice that the new page on the wall calendar needed turning. It was as though what was being discussed in class was insignificant, and what held primordial meaning, was the minutia that surrounded us—the push pins under my desk, the staples lodged in the rug, the tiniest flecks of paint on the wall, the fly on the window pane. His eyes were drawn to the smallest parts of our visual panorama, and like magnifying field binoculars, they scanned the school for treasures that he hurried to stash away into his pockets.

Nothing on the floor, or wall ever escaped this boy, yet he couldn't spell, his reading was halting, he couldn't grasp the concept of multiplication, or follow our simple directions for fire drills.

Because I had concerns about Jack's learning needs, I met with his parents, the principal, and our school learning specialist. Was his inability to follow what was going on in class due to a language processing disability? What about his attentional difficulties? How could I help him?

Jack underwent extensive testing, and the recommendations from the learning specialist enabled us to better provide for his educational needs. He started to see a tutor twice a week after school.

Yet, I still worried about his sense of self, and his lack of investment at school. He wasn't your typical class clown, however, the passive disruptions he provoked at school drew the attention of his peers, our principal, secretary, and other teachers. I had to find what motivated Jack.

The best way I've always known to gain the trust of children, was to become interested in what interested them.

It wasn't difficult with Jack. He had a passion. He loved baseball, everything about baseball, but especially the cards. The boy who collected paper and string at school, had managed to amass for himself a fine collection of baseball cards which he brought to school for math one day when we shared our collections with one another.

Many boys came to school carrying their card collections in heavy vinyl-covered albums bursting at the seams. But not Jack. He came in with an old battered shoe box that he held most lovingly against his chest. And once he opened it, the magic began. The boy who couldn't follow most of what was happening at school showed me how he had organized his cards by teams—the Yankees, the Braves, the Red Sox, the Orioles, the A's, the Reds—

and how he had wrapped his most valuable cards with elastic bands, and kept his holograms in an envelope at one end of the box. Jack had a system. There was order and organization in his collection.

"Now look at this card here, my Grandpa bought it for me when I was five. Look, look, I've got this magazine, it's where I check the value of my cards." Jack, who could barely read in class, was flipping through the magazine with its lists of football celebrities and card price tags, and laboriously reading out to me from the smallest font ever, the monetary value of some of his cards.

Jack's collection gave us something to talk about in the weeks to come. Every Wednesday when I walked the school playground on lunch duty, or while we climbed up the stairs on the way back from recess, or in the hallway first thing in the morning while he hung his coat, Jack was sure to accost me with an anecdote about baseball. We were beginning to develop a relationship, mostly a baseball relationship, but at least we had a common language.

One day during social studies, while the children were working on a map of California, Jack raised his hand. It was a chilly foggy morning, so I was wondering which window Jack was going to recommend we shut, or what extraneous thing he had noticed in the room. I moved closer to him, so he could whisper his question, and not disturb the other children. However, he surprised me with a question related to our mapping work.

"Can I go over my map with a black pen after I finish drawing it with pencil?"

"Yes, that's a good idea, Jack!"

I had to capitalize on it. "Children, may I have your attention, please? Jack came up with a fine idea." I turned to him. "Jack, tell them what you just asked me." He stood up, and with lips twitching into a smile, he repeated his question and my answer.

This trivial incident was a turning point for Jack. This was the first time he was viewed by his classmates as someone whose contribution was valuable, and worthy of our attention. Now they saw that Jack had good ideas, and that Mona thought so, too.

After this first incident, I continued to broadcast Jack's suggestions in an attempt to present him as a highly regarded member of our class community. And slowly he didn't need to solicit his friends' reactions by rolling his eyes, or wobbling his head, or falling off his chair. Instead, people were beginning to respect him for his ideas. He began to view himself as someone of value.

Jack needed a new role, he needed to feel useful. Because he loved animals, and had a dog, two cats and a guinea pig at home, and because I saw him often chatting with our classroom pet rats, Mickey and Pluto, I asked him to assist me every Thursday after school when I cleaned their cage. Jack was perfect for the job. He would hold Mickey and Pluto lovingly inside his sweatshirt while I emptied out their litter. Sometimes he made them mazes in the block corner, and gave them directions to follow in the maze. He talked to them as though they were his children, kindly, but firmly. He would refill their water bottle, and pour grain nuggets in their food dish.

I knew his job meant a lot to him; he couldn't wait till Thursday. Several times in the week, he'd ask me if it was Thursday yet, or drag me to the cage to point out how much it needed cleaning. It wasn't just the job, or even the beloved rats that made him wait impatiently, but it was also the relationship we had developed as we worked and talked together in the quiet of the room. Jack had a responsibility he took seriously, and a growing attachment to me.

At about that same time I had noticed that several children, including Jack, were distracted from doing independent work at their round tables of four. Every day at Writers' Workshop half of the class wanted an individual quiet place to work alone. The couple of old desks on the periphery of the room were being fought over by the children. What was I going to do?

I decided to write an entry in our class meeting notebook, and consult with the children.

Dear Slippery Lizards,
I noticed that some people can stay focused during independent work time, but that others get very distracted, and can't get their work done. Let's talk about it. Perhaps together we can find solutions that will help.

Love, Mona

The children seemed anxious at first, but I took a few minutes to expand on my entry, giving them examples of what I had noticed. Then they were pleased that I reflected for them their need for solitary work places. They all wanted to lament on their woes.

"I can't concentrate with other kids at my table."

"Every time Lauren and Tim open their folders, or you know, get their glue sticks, or something, I stop what I'm doing to watch them, and then I get all confused about my stuff."

"I can't focus when the kids at my table keep getting up to go sharpen their pencils, or get a tissue. I mean, I'm in the middle of writing a sentence, then someone gets up, and like, I lose my thoughts, or something."

"I wish I had my own spot so no one can disturb me."

"I really want to get my story finished, but I can't with all this stuff happening around me, you know, like people moving around, or talking."

"Okay, I hear you loud and clear. Now let's see how well you know yourselves. I'm going to ask you two questions. See which one best applies to you. The first one is, who has an easy time remaining focused on a project? Take your time before answering, and be as honest as you can."

Many hands went up. Some were unequivocal "yes's," while others went up and down, or wavered a bit as though unsure of themselves.

"Thank you. I really appreciate your honesty. Put your hands down. Now, question number two, tell me, who in this class would like to be able to focus better?"

Without any hesitation, and completely unabashedly, six hands went up. The same six children whom I had identified to myself as easily distractible. Among them was Jack.

"Why can't we have more work alone desks?" asked Nina readjusting her glasses on her nose.

"Yeah, that way we won't fight over them every day," said Ben.

"Well, let me see what I can do, but I need to know who thinks he or she might need an individual desk?"

Eight children responded.

"I'm very proud of you. You know what it is that you need, and I happen to agree with you. I, too, have noticed that you guys could use some quiet space."

After the meeting I wondered where I could ever find six more desks. I scrounged around in the school basement, and found three dusty desks stacked up in the corner. The teacher next door loaned me one wooden table. And finally I discovered two perfect matching tables at a garage sale.

With my six extra tables, I spent the weekend setting up my classroom to accommodate individual desks. The room didn't look as spacious, but I knew my students wouldn't mind.

On Monday the children rushed in the door buzzing around with excitement. Of course, everyone wanted a work alone place. We met on the rug to discuss the new classroom set-up.

"Children, you can see how popular those desks are! Let me reassure you. Everyone who needs a work alone place will eventually get one. But let me first ask you some questions. Raise your hand if you really, really need one now."

The same six hands went up.

"Fine. Now, who needs one, but it doesn't have to be right away? Who can wait a bit?"

A few hands were raised.

"Okay, and finally, who doesn't need a work alone space at all?"

The rest of the class responded.

Therefore, based on our discussion and vote, the children with the most urgent need got work alone desks first. They were to occupy them for one month. Then we would have another class discussion to see who needed work alone spaces, and give other children a chance to sit at those desks.

Jack was among the six children who felt they immediately needed a desk, and he was thrilled to have his own space. I made sure to place him near the front of the room which helped improve his involvement. He began to raise his hand to respond to questions, and stopped commenting on the room temperature, or the insects on the wall.

A few weeks later I announced to the children that they would each select a topic of their choice to research and write about.

In no time Jack had made up his mind. He was going to write "The Ultimate Book on Baseball."

And Jack, who used to meander the halls in search of something more worthwhile to do than to come to class, became one of the first children each morning to reach our door. He would excitedly pull out from his backpack several books on baseball that he had brought from home, and he borrowed more books from our school library than anyone else. Not only did he spend numerous hours reading baseball manuals and the biographies of Hank Aarons, Jackie Robinson and Babe Ruth, but he also wished to share his books and research with his classmates.

It was upon Jack's instigation that we instituted the daily ritual of "Research Presentations." At the end of every research period, many children volunteered to stand up in front of the class, and present, in an informal and impromptu fashion, the most recently acquired tidbits and facts they had read about that day. We soon had to put up a sign-up on the board, and limit the presentations to two minutes.

And reliably Jack was signing up every day to stand up in front of the whole class with his tattered reams of paper and scribbled notes to tell us something new and amazing about baseball.

"Did you know that when Babe Ruth was a little kid, he was so tough, like he used to throw rocks at delivery carts, and do things like that, so his parents sent him to an orphanage?...The New York Yankees won the most World Series...Guess who hit the most home runs in a season?"

One day while the children were writing their reports, a large maintenance vehicle with a long yellow crane attached to its side, drove onto our school grounds to carry and grind up some large eucalyptus limbs. Hearing the commotion, all the children rushed to the windows. So I decided we'd have a five-minute break from our work to watch the crane's maneuvers. No point in insisting that the children continue to write when such an exciting thing was happening right outside our windows!

When our five minutes were up, everyone settled back to work, except for Jack. I watched him struggle between his desire to write his baseball report, and the temptation to peek out the window. Finally, he came over to me, looking defeated, and told me how hard it was to get his work done.

"Jack, do you think it's the sound of the crane, or seeing it that distracts you the most?" I asked.

"I dunno." He shook his head.

"I wonder if you couldn't do a little experiment. Move your desk closer to the bookcase, and turn it around so you face the books in the shelves instead of the windows. Then notice if you can remain focused without seeing the crane. If you can't, then maybe it's the sound that bothers you, and I can get you some headphones to wear. They'll help keep some of the sound out."

With renewed vigor, Jack rushed over to his desk, and turned it around to face the bookcase. After a few minutes, I glanced in his direction, and saw him working away. Only occasionally did he turn his head toward the window.

It had been a lesson in self-awareness. That day Jack learned that he had the control to make changes that could help him learn better, that he could experiment and examine what worked best for him.

Jack's investment in school was not constant. Since we couldn't study baseball all year, he lost interest when we turned to other curriculum areas. It was hard for him to maintain the focus and involvement.

Every September the children make time capsules out of paper towel tubes in which they roll up a self-portrait, and a list of "Stuff About Me." They enjoy drawing themselves, and writing about themselves. I ask them to answer two questions: What am I good at? And what are my hopes for this year? When they're all done, they seal their tubes with tissue paper, and decorate them with ornaments, feathers and sequins, and then we stash them away for the year in a box on the top shelf of my closet. We don't see them again until June.

The last week of school we talk about our year together, what we've learned, and how we've changed. But before opening our time capsules, the children do a repeat of the fall, a self-portrait, what they're good at now, and how the year went for them. After they're done, they open their time capsules, and compare their September and June drawings and writing. It is a time of jubilation as the children see how much they've improved.

"Look, Mona, I used to draw so bad! I didn't even make ears or eyebrows on myself!" exclaimed Erin.

"Mona! Mona! I can't believe how bad I used to spell! Look, I spelled "writing" without a "w'!" shouted Pasong.

The children exchanged their work, and I heard lots of ooh's and aah's, giggles and shrieks.

Jack sat quietly gazing at his papers. I came over and sat next to him.

"What did you notice?" I asked.

He handed me his two self-portraits. The September one showed a tiny boy with red hair, big feet and big ears, his face covered with dots. He was standing at the plate, holding his bat, ready to hit. His list of what he was good at was short. One word, baseball.

In his June self-portrait, Jack had drawn himself as a full-size boy. He was standing in the classroom a huge smile from ear to ear, with Mickey on his shoulder while Pluto was peeking through a maze on the rug. Below the picture, he had written:

I'm good at:
1. drawing maps of California
2. reading
3. rat trainer
4. writing reports
5. and of course, baseball expert.

CHAPTER FOUR

Learning About Friendship

Sharing Friends

"Shireen won't let Nina have other friends. She bugs Heather, and pushes Kate around."

— Nina, Kate, and Heather

The day before class meeting, I read to myself our journal entry. Aha! The age-old problem of exclusion! Children know too well the sting of rejection when rebuffed with the dreaded words: "You can't play," or "You can't come to my birthday party." These words have the power of a life sentence. They can instantly send us into exile.

Shireen couldn't allow Nina to have other friends. Last year Nina had become best friends with Latoya. They were not maliciously exclusive, but like newlyweds, they were eternally preoccupied with each other. So everyone in the class admired them from a distance, knowing that having such strong feelings took up all of their energy.

However, Shireen could not stay away, nor read Nina and Latoya's social cues. She repeatedly attempted to thrust herself between the happy couple, only to find herself ignored or snubbed.

Yet now that Latoya had moved to a different school, the coast was clear, and Shireen felt entitled to step in and take her place. I was hoping that she and Nina could become friends, though I had my doubts.

Nina was a mature, portly eight-year-old. Her straight blonde hair fell down to her shoulders, and framed a serious, almost adult face. She wore small wire-rimmed glasses which, in her inattentiveness, she often misplaced in the classroom. She was a respected member of our class who was articulate when it came to expressing her feelings, and could easily resolve her own conflicts. Children sought her out for her wisdom, and her sense of justice. Nina's home life was not perfect, but stable. She had a little sister, Phoebe, and together they spent one week with each divorced parent. Ken was a chef, Carol worked in an office, and they provided their children with loving homes where the girls were trusted and respected. It showed in Nina's attitude and confidence at school.

Shireen, on the other hand, was unsure of herself. Almost a whole year younger than Nina, she had strived to be her equal, only to repeatedly fall short. Shireen was a big black girl with broad shoulders and a large waist. Her black hair, attached to colorful barrettes, was neatly braided into thin coils that rested on top of her head. Being large physically made her appear older than her age, yet her soft baby voice made her sound younger.

Shireen's relationships with other children were fraught with arguments. She desperately wanted to be noticed and loved, but every one of her attempts led to disappointment and rage. There had been daily tears the previous year. Was this going to be another year of feuding friendships and hurt feelings?

Shireen's home life was chaotic. Her mother, Yvonne, loved her very much, but the vicissitudes of their lives took a toll on Shireen. Yvonne was a single parent raising her three children alone—Raymond, Shireen, and Malcom, the baby. Raymond was an angry twelve-year-old, looking in the streets for the father he didn't have at home. During the day Yvonne worked at a shoe store, and at night she took classes at the local community college. She aspired to become a nurse. In order to cut down on housing costs, she had moved in with her widowed father, Julius. Julius was in his late seventies, a cranky old man who, I understood from Yvonne, never took a liking to Shireen, but adored the baby. Even though Yvonne recognized that her father was often impatient with Shireen, they continued to live with him. There were no easy answers for Yvonne.

I remembered how much I learned about Shireen's life from the day I dropped her off at her house after an all-day field trip to the beach. She was thrilled that I was driving her home, and begged me to come inside the house. "Please, please, I want you to see my kitten, Dotty! She's so cute!"

I came out of the car, and immediately felt vulnerable as I walked up to the front door and noticed that metal bars had been installed on the front door and windows of the little wooden Victorian house. Across the street was a neglected vacant yard strewn with empty beer bottles and McDonald paper wrappers. A small liquor store sat at the corner with a Budweiser neon sign blinking in the window.

I followed Shireen up the wooden stairs to the front porch where a child's bicycle stood tied to a column. "Do you ride your bike around the neighborhood?" I asked, realizing half-way through my sentence how naive my question was. She shook her head hard, "No, my mom won't let me, 'cuz sometimes there's shootings out there." She pointed to the liquor store.

Inside, the house was cluttered with dark furniture. I felt as though I had opened the door of a musty old attic with its stagnant air, and stale odor. A moosehead was hanging over the mantelpiece, and several trophies adorned the dining-room buffet—trophies, Shireen explained, from the days when in his youth Julius had played basketball in high school.

Yvonne came out of the kitchen carrying a chubby, wiggly Malcom on her hip. Julius followed—a tall, stooped man leaning on his cane, with hands gnarled like redwood burls. He wore a beret over his head and thick glasses with lenses that distorted his eyes.

Shireen was telling me the stories behind each trophy, when I overhead Julius talking to Yvonne about me, his voice deep and husky.

"Why she here, huh? What she come see? How poor black folks live?" I knew the questions were not meant for me, but I chose to respond.

"I didn't come to check out Shireen's house..."

"Oh, Daddy, quit being an ogre!" interjected Yvonne with a frustrated grin. "Where are your manners?"

Julius smiled, and hobbled on his cane to approach me and Shireen. Gently he lifted the tallest golden trophy, and stroked it without saying a word.

"That's Grandpa's favorite," whispered Shireen with sparkling eyes. "It's when he won the tournament."

"You've got quite a collection here, Mr. Jefferson!"

"Oh, yes!" he sang with a charming southern drawl. "We was the best."

Shireen dragged me away from Julius to show me the room she shared with Raymond and Malcolm. She disturbed Dotty from a nap under the bed, and placed her in my arms. That's when Yvonne invited me to join them in the kitchen for a snack. Together we drank apple juice in tall plastic cups from McDonald's, and ate wedges of pears around the vinyl-covered kitchen table.

Shireen had told me at school that her grandfather had grown up picking cotton in Alabama, so I asked him to tell me about his childhood. And he obliged with relish. He told me he was the oldest child in a family of seven boys. He had to do chores around the house, and help his Mama take care of his little brothers.

"Come rain or shine, we walked three miles each way to go to school. Sometimes we was wearin' no shoes."

"You had to walk a long way to school while the white kids rode the school bus. Right?" I asked.

At first Julius stared at me, then I saw a faint smile forming on his face.

That afternoon Julius and I got along just fine. It was easy to see that he had had a hard life. I wanted to ask him many questions about his experiences in the South, and his move to California, but I held my peace. I gathered that the only way he knew how to deal with frustration and anger was to yell at Shireen.

• • •

Back at our class meeting, the children sat around me on the rug as I read Nina's entry.

"Nina, tell us about this incident," I asked, noting that she had written it in the third person.

She nodded with a dignified look on her face, and started to give us a brief history of her relationship with Shireen. She mentioned the painful triangle with Latoya last year, and all the unsuccessful efforts at becoming friends with Shireen. I knew what she was saying—I had seen it, too.

"Nina?" I asked. "Do you think Shireen might be wanting to be your exclusive friend?"

Nina didn't get a chance to answer. Heather jumped in, "Shireen won't even let *me* be friends with Nina!"

Heather was a reserved child, tall and skinny, with a pale, narrow face tilted sideways like the women in Modigliani's paintings. Her thin brown hair was parted to one side, and often obscured half of her face. She had known Nina all her life, their mothers were close friends. Though the girls had played at each other's houses, they had never been best friends at school.

Before I could ask any further questions, Shireen spoke in a soft, slow, deliberate voice.

"Nina and I were playing on the swings, then she went off to play with Heather and Kate."

"And how did that make you feel?"

"Bad." Her eyes lowered. Then she added, "The girls said, 'Let's not be near her, let's never talk to her,'" she mimicked with a swaying motion of her head.

"We never said that!" exploded Nina. Heather and Kate looked offended.

I wanted to be fair as I listened to my students' stories, but their stories didn't match. Perhaps, the answer lay in the moment of not matching.

Kate offered, "Heather plays at Nina's house, but she never gets a chance to be Nina's friend at school." Kate was good at reflecting other children's sorrows. She was a petite child, small-boned and frail-looking with dark curly hair. Even though serious most of the time, she liked to flash you a purposeful smile to show off her glittering braces.

"Last year Shireen didn't want me to be friends with Latoya. I feel it's starting all over again," said Nina, her voice cracking as she tried to contain the tears.

The class wanted to speak. Everyone had experienced wanting a special friend. I felt stumped.

"Does anyone have ideas that can help the girls get along?" I asked.

Ben volunteered, "They can ask each day before starting to play how they want to do it."

"We do that already, and we have a lot of fights. Plus, you can say no to a friend once in a while, but not every day," Nina quickly objected.

Jeremiah, who was boisterous and fidgety, suggested, "Maybe you can take turns deciding who you want to play with." He swayed and rocked, barely keeping himself anchored to the rug.

"We tried that, but it didn't work," said Heather nonchalantly.

The girls were picky, and I was getting annoyed. Ben and Jeremiah had come up with some good suggestions only to have them be turned down immediately. I wanted to ask the girls to reconsider, but I decided to be patient, knowing that I couldn't wrap things up quickly according to my own time frame.

I turned to Jessica and Sofia who had had a similar problem with Shireen last week, but had not entered it in the class notebook. I happened to have witnessed it get resolved on the playground.

"How did you resolve it?" I asked.

"We had a rotation," said Sofia. "One day Shireen played with us, the next day me and Jessica played alone, and on and on."

"How did that work for you?"

"Not too good," answered Jessica. "We didn't like it...mmm...that we couldn't be free to play any way we wanted." Jessica's speech was often punctuated with pauses and mmm's.

"I think we should try the rotation way," interjected Kate. "It's better than all this fighting. Shireen and Nina can play alone one day, then the next day we can all play together."

"Shireen, what do you think about this plan?" I asked, relieved that a solution was in sight. "Do you want to try playing one day alone with Nina, and then one day with everyone?"

She didn't like the idea, neither did Nina.

We were at a standstill. I could feel my frustration making its way into the meeting. A moment ago I began to feel defeated, when Nina had said, "It's starting all over again." Having to face the hopelessness of Shireen and Nina's friendship at the beginning of the year, when one normally anticipates hope, deflated my optimism and enthusiasm.

"Children," I said. "You know, we didn't choose each other as a class. We came together by fate. It's just plain luck that we are in this class together. Some of us are quiet, some are loud, some are active, some are less active, some are sure of themselves, others are unsure. We're all very different. We've got a whole year to learn how to live together. Do you think we can do it?"

I felt as though I was rallying the troops. I heard an enthusiastic "Yes, Mona!"

"It will take time, but we can start today. Let's give it our best. Let's continue to talk about this problem next time. We're all learning from it."

I wasn't totally convinced that we could make it work, because last year Shireen had been the class victim. I wondered whether she had taken on that role for herself, or whether she had been assigned that role by her classmates. I remembered last year's daily frustrations, and now I felt ashamed and sad at having been unable to make it different for her.

I had tried to protect the beginning sparks of friendship I saw develop between Shireen and some of the other girls, encouraging friendly partnerships during work periods and inviting her to co-author books with other children. Alas, most of my attempts were unsuccessful. Completely unaware of it, she sabotaged her chances to make friends. She'd disagree with someone's suggestion, make a derogatory remark about someone's lunch box or jacket, or refuse to scoot over on the bench to make room for a friend.

Unfortunately, I seldom witnessed any of these altercations—they happened in a hush and away from the scrutiny of others. But sooner or later Shireen's friends came to me in tears to complain about how she had mistreated them. Subsequently, the fights she had initiated with other children had the effect of excluding her from their play.

Could Shireen withstand another year of rejection? What could I do to help her see the effects of her behavior, and recover from those injuries? How could I help her make friends?

The Singing Club

"Nina, Heather, Erin, and Kate had a singing club. We practiced for days for the potluck. Then Shireen asked if she could join, but she hadn't practiced. So we said no. Shireen went to tell Sofia all about it, and Sofia came up, and said to us, "You guys are crazy."

— Nina, Heather, Erin, and Kate

It had only been a week since I'd dismissed the class meeting with my cheerleading pep-talk. "Yes, Mona!" they had shouted, buoyed by my request to learn to live together peacefully. And here we were today, faced again with the same old problem of exclusion.

"Nina, tell us what happened," I asked, trying not to sound disheartened.

Nina explained that Shireen had made fun of the singing club at recess, teasing the girls about their voices. Then when they decided to perform at the school family potluck, Shireen insisted she wanted to join. However, because she hadn't practiced, the girls rejected her request.

"Shireen kept putting her hands over her ears when we practiced," Heather added. "She said she hated our singing. Well, then, I'd like to know, in the first place, why she wanted to join our club?"

"Because she wanted to get to sing at the potluck," answered Kate, who could easily see someone else's perspective, and who, at that moment, sounded very understanding of Shireen.

"Who planned this performance?" I asked, completely unaware of a scheduled singing performance slated for our potluck.

"We did," said Nina. "We thought it would be nice to sing some songs for the parents after we finish eating."

"Shireen," I asked, "tell us what you remember of this incident."

"Well, I wanted to join the singing club, and they said no. I asked really nice." Her speech softened as she said, "Can I join your club?" And then she added in a harsh tone of voice, "And they said, 'No!'"

"But Shireen," Kate interjected, "you hadn't practiced with us!"

"I knew the words of those songs, anyway!"

"You did not!" replied Nina and Kate in unison.

This discussion had a familiar ring. We were heading toward the zone where stories don't match.

I looked at all the girls involved, and asked, "Could Shireen have been part of the club even without knowing the words?"

Erin raised her hand. She hadn't spoken yet. Even though younger and smaller than the rest of the girls, she was respected by her peers.

"Shireen, we didn't want to exclude you. Remember when we asked you if you wanted to be master of ceremonies instead of singing, and introduce our songs to the audience, and you said no?"

Shireen sighed as if there were no point fighting. At that moment I wanted to wrap my arm around her shoulder, and comfort her.

"You did not want to be master of ceremonies?" I guessed.

"No, I did not."

I found myself torn between the need to wrap up the girls' problem into a tidy package, and my awareness that I'd be robbing them of the opportunity to learn how to negotiate. Did the girls purposefully exclude Shireen, and if so, what had been their reason? Was she an innocent victim? Or did she provoke them in some way?

"Children, clubs can be a problem sometimes. Can you tell me why?" I wanted to include everyone. Children know the power of inviting a new member to a club, or rejecting one. All children know how it feels to be included or excluded.

"When you have a club, kids always argue 'bout who's gonna be president of the club."

"Someone always bosses everybody around."

"It's hard to agree."

"Some clubs don't let other kids join."

"There are lots of fights."

"So what I'm hearing from you today, is that it can be hard belonging to a club, because issues of power and control can come up. It's not easy to be fair, and share the power among all the members of a club. And you know what? It's hard even for adults who belong to a club or a committee. Adults can get bossy, or exclusive; some do a lot of work, while others do nothing. It's also important to have a fair leader, someone you can trust, someone who listens to the rest of the group, someone who doesn't boss everyone around, but who is kind, and firm and easy to get along with."

"Mona, I don't think clubs work when it's all kids the same age," said Kate. "You know why it works to make decisions in class? It's because you're our teacher, so you have the authority." With her clear and direct words, Kate had spoken like a prophet. The class was impressed.

"Well, why do you think it works when I help you make a decision, when I 'have the authority' as Kate said?"

"We trust you, that's why," said Nicko.

"You're strict...mmm, but you're fair at the same time," said Jessica.

"You listen to us, even when we complain," added Sofia.

"We know you real good, Mona," smiled Pasong.

"So are you telling me that you need to know your leaders well, that they need to be trustworthy, firm and fair, and that they need to listen to the group. Is that what I'm hearing you say?"

Heads were nodding.

Then Nina spoke with her usual insight. "Yeah, it's like when we voted in class about what kinds of vegetables to grow in our garden. Nobody had a fit if his idea didn't win. Kids accepted it. But when we make decisions in our clubs and vote, kids make a big scene and cry if they don't get their way."

"Children, it's almost time for lunch. I think it's helping all of us to identify what works and what doesn't work in clubs. We have started a good discussion about what makes for a good leader. Let's continue soon."

Impossible to have resolved a monumental problem such as this one in forty-five minutes! Maybe it helped the children become aware that dialogues can continue, and that realistically speaking, problems don't get resolved in one single sitting.

The following week at our school family potluck, Shireen, grinning with obvious pleasure, stood in the company of the girls, singing in front of an audience of parents and siblings. Her round face shone with pride as she sang our repertoire of songs, from *Clementine* to *Yellow Submarine*. She was definitely a part of the gang.

The next day, when I asked the girls how they had resolved the problem, no one really knew. Perhaps they had forgiven Shireen for her previous insulting comments about their voices. Perhaps our talk about leaders had alerted the girls to the abuse of power that can exist in clubs. Or perhaps still, the group had worked it out the way I remember working things out as a child—the next day things are forgotten, and you just go on with your life as though nothing had happened.

What Is a Friend?

"I got on a swing, then Shireen ran up and said, 'I want that swing.' I said, 'Count to 50.' And Shireen said, 'No, 25.' At that point I said, 'A real friend wouldn't say that.' Then when I was sitting around, I saw Jessica crying because Shireen didn't listen to her, and I thought, 'That does it!'"

— Nina

At our school if all the swings are being used, and you'd like a turn, you let one of the users know, and you start counting to fifty. At fifty, the user of the swing has to get off, and let you have your turn. It's always worked, because the children themselves had developed that rule after frustrating disputes over the use of the swings.

I still remember the day, a few years ago, when that rule was created. It was a week or two into September when the children came thundering into the classroom after lunch, red in the face with anger.

"What do you want to do?" I'd asked. "What can best help you maintain fairness at the swings?"

And the children had shouted what I had hoped to hear, "Rules, Mona, rules!"

"All right, what are some possibilities? Let's brainstorm together."

And they had unanimously voted in favor of counting to 50. It sounded fair to them, and it has worked just fine ever since.

At the beginning of the year, I don't talk about classroom rules, because I believe that when children create their own rules, they are more likely to respect them, and get involved in their implementation. Yet, some of my colleagues worry that I don't have a set of classroom rules posted on the wall to serve as a visual reminder to the children.

"How will your students know what is right and what is wrong? How will you be able to set limits?" they ask with the best of intentions. Good questions, but year after year, my answer remains the same.

"Do you keep a list of family rules hanging on your kitchen wall? No, you don't. And that's because your rules are, to a certain extent, internalized by your family members. It would be almost offensive, and somewhat ludicrous to read, 'Remember to say Please and Thank You,' or 'Do not tease your little sister!' In the same way, I want our classroom to become a community, like a family, where people create rules as they encounter problems, and where the rules are known internally by everyone."

Starting day one, I tell the children we're going to create a community in our classroom. Then I ask them what they think that could mean. They say, "We're going to be kind to each other, work well together, help one another."

Then day by day we start to live together. And it is in this living together day by day that we encounter our first problems. Slowly they realize that it is out of chaos that rules are made to protect the rights of each and every member of the community.

Nina was following the rules on the swings. So was Shireen, because the kindergartners who use the same playground we do, counted to 25 at the swings, 50 being too high a number for some of them. Even though Shireen was a third-grader, she often played at recess with younger children, and must have assumed that counting to 25 at the swing was the golden rule for everyone.

"Nina, tell us about the incident at the swings," I asked after reading her entry to the class.

"I mean, if I was swinging and, say Heather wanted to get on, she wouldn't tell me, 'No, 25,'" Nina imitated Shireen's high-pitched voice. "A good friend doesn't argue with you like that. A good friend trusts you."

"Shireen, what do you think about that?"

She kept her head bowed as she spoke, and there was no expression in her voice, "I counted to 25. I was doing the right thing. I...I was...I was following the rules."

The girls were talking about two different things. Is that what happens when two people have a disagreement? Two levels of conversation that don't connect? Nina was talking about trust and friendship, Shireen about rules and justice.

"You both have valid points, but can you see that you're talking about two different things? Shireen about rules, Nina about being a good friend." The girls felt understood by me, but I wasn't sure they understood each other yet.

I added, "Let's first talk about the most practical aspect of this problem—swing rules."

We discussed how to be fair on the swings, and we arrived at a happy agreement. From now on, everyone would count to 25, so there'd be consistency among all the children in our school. I would discuss it with the other teachers. The children were relieved—there would be no more confusion.

"Nina, let's get back to the rest of the problem you wrote up in the notebook. What did you mean by 'That does it!'?"

"Well, see, I was upset by what happened with Shireen on the swings, then I saw Jessica upset because Shireen had walked away without listening, so I got mad at her. I've had it with the way Shireen acts around here. You know, she says she wants to be our friend, but then she doesn't act like one."

Nina had spoken with vehemence, her eyes brimming with tears, as though she couldn't keep the hurt locked up inside her any longer. I wondered if she knew that, in this moment of feeling betrayed by Shireen, she was probably missing Latoya.

What would have been the point in confronting Shireen for her lack of friendship toward Nina or Jessica? Shireen and Nina were speaking different languages. What Shireen needed most was to feel safe at school in order to get along better with her classmates.

"Since we're talking about friendship, children, tell me, what do you look for in a good friend?"

"Someone who's nice."

"Someone who helps you, like if your lunch box opens up and your lunch falls out on the ground, a good friend would help you pick it up."

"Someone who makes you feel better when you're sad."

"Someone you can trust, who won't go and tell on you."

"Someone who plays with you, like when you're lonely, they'll say, 'Do you want to play?'"

The children wanted their friends to treat them well, to help them, be kind, and respect them. Their requests were not unreasonable. Yet, why are childhood friendships so often plagued with disputes and tears?

Because there was still enough time to tackle one more problem before lunch, and because the next problem was connected to this last one, I decided to continue.

Problem #2

"When Shireen asked to get onto the tire swing, I said no. She told me I had to. I tried to explain to her that she always makes it go in swirls very fast."

— Jessica

Nina's problem led us right into Jessica's. Jessica was a shy, lanky, old-fashioned girl who looked like she belonged to the world of Laura Ingalls Wilder's frontier life. She had blonde hair which was carefully braided, pensive blue eyes, and a narrow chin that jutted out a bit. She would have resembled the paper dolls of my childhood had it not been for the colorful striped leggings she liked to wear.

Jessica didn't like to talk much in class. It might have been due to her halting speech that was interspersed with many "mmm's," but I suspected that her silence was also indicative of her thoughtful, observing nature. I wondered how clear and fluent her speech would be under the duress of a class meeting.

"Jessica, what happened that day on the tire swing?"

"Well," she started, "I tried to explain...mmm...to Shireen...mmm..., but she walked away."

"Tell us some more about the swirling very fast."

"Well, you see...mmm...Shireen likes to...make the tire swing go...mmm...round and round. And...mmm...it gives me a headache." Jessica spoke with her hands a lot.

"I know that some people get dizzy easily, and can get sick to their stomach," I offered. "I have that problem when I ride the roller coaster."

Immediately some of the children wanted to volunteer their roller coaster stories. I called on a few children, because I wanted Jessica to know that she wasn't alone in feeling dizzy, and for Shireen to hear someone else's point of view.

"Shireen, did you know that Jessica didn't like it when you swirled the tire swing very fast?"

"No," answered Shireen, sulking.

Jessica didn't wait for an invitation to speak. This time she lunged without pauses or mmm's, "Well, you would have known if you hadn't walked off, you know! You didn't want to listen."

"Yes," interjected Nina, "that's when I found Jessica crying in the playground."

Shireen was fuming. "You were being mean to me," she blasted at Jessica. "You yelled at me, so I didn't wanna stay 'round."

"Okay, Shireen," I tried to calm her down. "You might have felt rejected when Jessica refused to have you join her on the swing, but don't you think it was your responsibility to find out why Jessica didn't let you ride with her?"

"She was yelling so loud, it was hurting my ears," Shireen covered her ears.

"I don't like it...that you cover your ears when...mmm...we're trying to tell you something," said Jessica.

I, too, had noticed that Shireen tended to cover her ears when in a conflict, even though the children were not always yelling at her. I had also noticed that she perceived even the slightest skin pressure as painful. She would shy away from a gentle pat on the back, and cry profusely at the slightest scratch. Could her hearing be sensitive, too, or was it more related to an avoidance technique, or a fear of being reprimanded, and having to take responsibility?

Sofia, Jessica's best friend, wanted to speak. She was a serious girl with saucy brown eyes, and hair pulled back into short black pigtails. "I was on the tire swing with Jessica when Shireen came over. I didn't like it that she walked away when Jessica tried to explain to her about swirling too fast."

"I wonder if it felt like someone slamming the door in your face," I ventured. Sofia and Jessica nodded.

"Let me tell you a story. When I was in fourth grade, there were two girls in my class who liked each other a lot, but who could also have the biggest fights: Charlotte and Deedee. Well, one day, Mira, another girl in our class who was jealous of Charlotte and Deedee's friendship, told Charlotte that Deedee didn't like Charlotte's new haircut, that she thought it was ugly."

The children were completely absorbed.

"So," I continued, "You can just imagine how Charlotte felt!"

A few children said, "Bad," even though I had not meant to elicit answers from them.

"Yes, Charlotte felt very bad to hear that Deedee didn't like her haircut. The next day when Deedee came to ask her to play, Charlotte walked away, pretending not to hear. Deedee ran after her, and repeated her question, but Charlotte pretended again not to hear."

"But why didn't she stop Charlotte," interrupted Ben, "and ask her to listen? I mean, it's pretty rude to walk away like that."

"Yeah, but Charlotte was angry," exclaimed Heather. "She thought Deedee had spoken behind her back to Mira about her haircut!"

"Well, maybe Mira lied. Remember she was jealous of Charlotte and Deedee's friendship," added Kate. "I think Charlotte shouldn't have walked away from Deedee. She should have given her a second chance."

Giving a friend a second chance. An option I often offered to the children. Now Kate was suggesting it as a tool in her repertoire of strategies for getting along with friends.

"Children, when you don't listen to your friends explain themselves, you hurt them and you hurt yourself. Can you guess why?" I asked.

"You hurt them, 'cause you don't give 'em a chance."

"It's rude and disrespectful to walk away, and that hurts their feelings."

"You hurt them, 'cause what if they've got something important to tell you."

The children could easily imagine how they could hurt someone else by walking away, but it was harder for them to understand how walking away was hurtful to them.

I decided to broach the subject myself. "Walking away is hurtful to you, because you miss out on making up with a friend, you don't get a chance to resolve your conflict, and you lose out on learning how to get along with other people. It's too bad Shireen was hurt by Jessica's rejection, but now Shireen knows Jessica was trying to explain to her that she doesn't like the swing to be swirled too fast."

"Maybe they can still swing together another day, and Shireen will know not to swirl the swing too fast," said Porter.

"But Mona, what happened to Charlotte and Deedee?"

"Charlotte finally told Deedee the whole story, and Deedee denied that she had said Charlotte's haircut was ugly. Did Deedee really say that about Charlotte's haircut, or did Mira make that story up to stir trouble? No one ever figured out the truth. The two girls played together the next day, and the next, but their friendship didn't end like a fairy tale. They didn't live happily ever after. They had many more fights. It's too bad they didn't know how important it is to trust, and listen to each other, even when what you have to listen to is difficult to hear."

"It's too bad they didn't have class meetings at your school, Mona!" exclaimed Kate, her eyebrows arching.

"Yes, I wish my teachers could have helped me and my friends get along better. But, you know what? I'm enjoying it vicariously through our class meetings!"

"What's vicca...resly?" puzzled Sofia.

"It means, 'I'm getting now through our class meetings what I wish I had received as a kid.'"

I gazed at Shireen, and wondered whether she would listen next time, and not walk away covering her ears, feeling like a victim. She desperately wanted to have friends, but she needed to be kind, and loyal, and flexible. Yet, I questioned whether she could do it when she didn't have any confidence in herself and her abilities? How could she trust the world when she didn't believe in herself? Hopefully, I was able to reach her with my story of Charlotte and Deedee.

I wondered, though, why I had chosen to tell this particular story. Was there something about the unsuccessful nature of Charlotte and Deedee's friendship? Was I beginning to realize that Shireen's problems couldn't resolve themselves peacefully because there was no trust?

Sometimes being in the presence of other people's miseries can get to you. I felt sad and just as defeated as Shireen must have felt. I felt as though I were standing outside a locked door unable to produce the right key.

Unloading the Baggage

Seven entries in the class notebook. Shireen had been the victim of seven crimes. They all had to do with some sort of injustice done to her—teasing, poking, pushing, hitting, screaming—injustices done to her by Pasong, Jeremiah, Porter, William, Lauren, and Erin. Not her usual group of girls.

I wanted Shireen to be involved in the process of reflecting on her behavior, so I asked, "I've noticed that you've had lots of problems this past week with different people. Have you noticed it, too?"

She nodded.

"Well, what do you say? What's going on?"

Did she see these repeated conflicts as isolated and accidental, or did she think she was being systematically victimized?

"Kids are being mean to me all the time," she murmured, looking demure and injured.

It looked to me, however, as though Shireen's classmates were treating her respectfully. Could it be, then, that the minute my back was turned, Shireen became the victim of their tyranny? And what if Shireen were manipulating us? Even though I always want to first believe the children, I was starting to feel fooled.

When children wrote several entries in the notebook during the course of one week, I gave them a chance to select their most pressing problem. However, today I had made the selection myself, based on the fact that I had overheard children saying that Erin was very worried about the class meeting. Foremost on my mind was wanting to alleviate Erin's fears, but I was also intrigued by this entry knowing that Erin was an overly polite, almost genteel girl.

I glanced at her before reading Shireen's entry. Erin was sitting next to Nina, her arms wrapped defensively around her body. I had a hard time imagining her screaming, yet the class notebook read:

"Erin was screaming at me when I was standing by her chair."

— Shireen

I told Shireen the reason I chose this problem, and I read the entry to the class. From the corner of my eye I could see Erin turning red in the face.

"Shireen, tell us what happened?"

"Well," she started, looking quite pleased with herself. "Erin screamed at me so loud that it hurt my ears." Smug smile. Again, words that didn't match the facial expression.

"Why did she scream at you? Did you ask?"

"I don't know." Shireen seemed almost inconvenienced by my question.

"Shireen, remember we've already discussed how it's your responsibility to ask. How can you begin to resolve your conflicts when you have no idea why people act the way they do?" I did not expect an answer, and Shireen must have known it since she remained silent, almost pouting.

I turned to Erin who was biting her lower lip so hard, it had turned crimson red.

"Erin, do you remember what happened that day?"

"Yeth," she said swallowing hard. She had the vestige of a lisp that made her sound like a preschooler. "Shireen was near where I was sitting, and all of a sudden she said to me, 'Erin, I'm going to write you up in the class notebook.' So I asked her, 'Shireen, would you please tell me what I did?' But she wouldn't answer me, and she walked away to get the notebook."

"Yes, I saw her..." started Nina.

"Nina," I interrupted. "Please wait until Erin and Shireen are finished, then the rest of the class can make comments or suggestions."

She nodded apologetically.

"Coming back to what you were saying, Erin, did you scream at Shireen, when she refused to answer and walked away?"

Erin's eyes darted frantically around the room. I thought she might have been considering dashing out the door. Finally she said yes as if she had been caught with a hand in the cookie jar.

"Erin, do you think it's okay to shout at someone when you're angry?" I asked.

"Oh, no! No!" she promptly replied, shaking her head for emphasis, licking her swollen, red lips, and looking contrite.

She seemed surprised when I turned to the class, and asked, "Children, do you sometimes shout when you're angry?"

Most hands went up, including my own.

"You're not alone, Erin. Look around you. Most of us shout sometimes when we're angry. It's quite normal."

She nodded fast with a repeated jerk of the head, but I could tell she wasn't completely relieved. "Well, at home, my mom doesn't like it when I shout," she managed to say in a whisper.

"Let's go back to the incident with Shireen. Why did you scream at her?" I asked, hoping to point out to Erin that she was entitled to be furious at Shireen.

"I screamed because she wouldn't answer me, and because I didn't know what I had done wrong."

"Shireen, what did Erin do?"

Shireen was taken aback. She had not expected my question. "She was whispering something behind my back to some other girls," she replied.

"I was not!" insisted Erin.

"She was not!" shouted furious voices in the room.

Pandemonium.

Here we go again! One story clashing against another. Did the girls say something about Shireen behind her back, or did Shireen assume they were talking about her? In fact, Shireen didn't care as much about Erin talking behind her back, as she did about the screaming. I'd known how sensitive she was to loud sounds, and that's what she chose to write about in the notebook.

Time to hear from the rest of the class, and the children were eager to talk. "Some of you seem to remember what happened that day?"

Nina spoke first. "I was sitting with Erin. I swear we weren't talking about Shireen or anything. Then suddenly she told Erin she was going to write her up in the notebook, and you know, she smiled when she started writing in the notebook. It was like she was glad to get Erin into trouble."

"Thank you. Does anyone else want to say anything?"

"I saw what happened," said Kate calmly. "It's like Shireen was enjoying torturing Erin by writing her up in the notebook without telling her why. I mean, Erin was very upset. I remember that."

"Thanks, Kate."

I turned to Nicko who was frantically waving his hand up in the air. "Yes, Nicko?"

"I saw Shireen writing in the notebook. I didn't know what the problem was about, but I saw Erin, you know, shouting, 'Tell me what I've done!'"

I thanked Nicko, then turned to Shireen. "What I'm hearing is that you didn't want to explain to Erin why you were writing her up in the notebook. Now, let me ask the class, what do you all think about that?"

"It wasn't fair to Erin. She couldn't even defend herself."

"I always want to know what people are mad at me about."

"It really makes me angry when people ignore me when I ask them something."

"Shireen didn't even ask Erin to solve it."

"Shireen could have told Erin the reason without torturing her like that. That was cruel."

"Sometimes I can't trust Shireen."

Although hard for Shireen to sit through this litany, it was important for her to hear what her peers had to say. The children had strong opinions on that matter, and everything they had to say made sense. Now it was my turn.

"Children, let's make sure this doesn't happen again. Let's today create a rule together: From now on, if you need to write in the notebook, you have to first try to solve your problem with the other person, and if that doesn't work, tell the other person, 'I can't resolve it with you right now. I'll write it up in the notebook so the whole class can help us.' But please don't use the notebook to intimidate other children, or threaten them, and have power over them. That's not going to help us create a community." I paused. "Does that make sense?"

The children agreed. They always seemed reassured when I made a proclamation to protect our community.

"Mona," Kate exclaimed. "Maybe Shireen needs her own notebook, you know, like Pasong has his own Dream Journal. Maybe Shireen can write her problems in her own book."

Kate had a good idea, yet I hesitated to give Shireen her own notebook. Knowing how special Pasong had felt when given his own journal made me worry that giving a journal to Shireen would take some of that specialness away from Pasong.

"Just a minute, Kate. I first want to ask Shireen a question." I turned to Shireen. "Do you understand that it wasn't okay to intimidate Erin with the notebook?"

With reservation, and no apparent contrition, Shireen agreed. What was it that made it difficult for her to understand Erin's rage?

"Shireen, you and I have noticed that you're using the class meeting notebook a lot. I'm wondering if some of these problems can't be dealt with right then and there, when they arise. There isn't enough time to deal with all of them at the meeting. Do you see that?"

"Yes."

As I was getting ready to address Kate's suggestion, I looked into Shireen's forlorn face, and I understood how much she needed rescuing. In that moment I realized that her gift couldn't take away from Pasong's, because it was different. It stemmed from her needs. It was hers.

"To come back to Kate's suggestion, I think it was a lovely idea! Shireen, would you like to have your own journal in which you could write about all the things that make you angry, or perhaps draw some angry pictures?"

Her dark brown eyes sparkled as her eyebrows arched, and her whole face perked up. "Yes, I'd like that very much." Then she added, "Sometimes in the morning my big brother hits me before I come to school."

Did she mention her brother because she was taking some responsibility for what was happening at school? Perhaps she was beginning to understand cause and effect, and that events are not isolated. Things weren't happening haphazardly. I was hoping she would start making connections, and take more responsibility.

"Maybe by writing or drawing about those things that make you angry or sad, you can get along better with your classmates. Maybe it would make it easier to be patient and kind, if you don't have to carry all your hurts around all day."

A big weight was lifted. There was hope.

The next day I provided Shireen with a personal journal—a small spiral-bound notebook with two playful kittens on the cover. Shireen, like Pasong, often wrote in it first thing in the morning. I came to call this ritual "Unloading the Baggage."

Solved

Our class meeting notebook seemed to have turned from a depository of hurt feelings to an arena for getting attention. I was beginning to question my creation.

Week after week the problems piled up in the notebook. I could barely keep up. Sometimes during the meeting, I'd lump together problems with similar themes in order to save time. Other times I'd ask the children involved to select only one problem, the most urgent. It made me uncomfortable to put off discussing the other problems. How could I be sure that one problem was more pressing than another? It was all a matter of conjecture. Too subjective, and definitely not reliable.

Why weren't my students starting to cope more successfully on their own? Perhaps addicted to our weekly meetings, they had stopped looking inside themselves for their own solutions. Perhaps they were clamoring for my attention the way siblings compete for their mother. I'd expected to see their growing independence and self-sufficiency. What had gone wrong?

Earlier in the year, when I had first introduced class meetings to the children, I had explained that if they were to solve a problem after having written it up, they could circle it, and write "Solved" over it. One rule: No erasing, because I wanted to keep a record of our problems, and congratulate them.

Now, three months into the school year, when I was frustrated and burdened by my confusion, and least expecting it, our first problem got solved independently of class meetings. It was signed by Nina, Kate, Heather and Erin.

I opened the notebook and smiled. "Children, today we need to celebrate."

They frowned, puzzled by my cheery remarks. Usually the beginning of our meetings were like the seconds before a bomb is detonated. The children's bodies were tight, the air heavy, the faces solemn. But today, I had taken them by surprise.

"We have our first independently-solved problem!"

I turned to Nina. "Shall I read it to the class?"

Nina looked at Kate, Heather and Erin. They made hesitant faces to each other while shaking their heads.

I intervened, "You know, girls, your problem can remain confidential. It's okay."

They nodded.

"Nevertheless, I want to congratulate the four of you, and the other person involved, for solving your problem on your own, and without requesting the assistance of class meeting. Tell me, was it hard?" There was no way these girls could have known how timely their solved entry was for me.

Kate and Erin immediately blurted out, "Yeah!"

Nina and Heather, who tended to be more resilient, kept quiet at first.

Then Nina said, "Well, it wasn't very easy, because we were really mad at this person in our class who did something..."

She paused to look at her friends, needing to check in with them, and get their approval.

Then she went on, "...And we started to yell at her, but then the next day we talked about it together and got over it."

I, of course, had read the mysterious entry, and knew that "this person in our class" was Shireen. I think everyone else knew it, too. Yet, no one glared at her. No one said a word.

Shireen's face was impassive. Did she know about the problem? Was she safer or more vulnerable because her name had not been mentioned? I wasn't sure.

"Would anyone else like to add something?" I was hoping that if Shireen needed to give her point of view, she'd have her chance.

Silence.

"Well, I hope this is only the beginning of many more independently-solved problems in our class."

My enthusiasm and encouragement worked. Maybe they'd traded in getting attention for lamenting, for getting attention for solving problems. Whatever the motivation, I was relieved to see a shift in our class. The following week the same four girls solved another problem with Shireen. And every week thereafter more and more students solved their own problems.

I had noticed that the girls, who were solving their own problems outside of class meetings, had acquired their own style of negotiation based on our class meeting procedures. They listened to one another better, and seemed to respect each other's differences.

One day, at a class meeting later in the school year, I asked them,

"I'm curious. Could you tell me why we don't seem to have as many problems written up by girls? Is it that girls have fewer problems than boys, or do girls solve their problems separately?"

Heather answered, "Well, we do have less problems now than we used to, but we also like to solve our problems on our own."

"How do you do that? Your strategies could be useful to the boys." Because we had created a safe classroom, I could make this comment and still know that the boys would listen without getting defensive.

Sofia told us that if they have a problem getting along at recess, they try to solve it the next day. For example, if a friend had felt excluded one day, then the next day they would make up a new role in their games to accommodate her.

Heather added that sometimes the next day, they don't know how it happens, but they seem to forget about their problem and everyone is happy again.

"Now correct me if I'm wrong. What you're really saying to me is that you either ignore small problems, or you change your ways to accommodate someone else. In other words, you either let things slide, or you become more flexible."

"Yeah!" They smiled.

"You know, this is just about how grown-ups take care of their own problems. Perhaps the boys can make use of your ideas. Thank you for sharing them with us."

For some students, solving their own problems offered new social possibilities, while for others, even this alluring benefit did not curb the need to jot down their complaints.

What if Nina, Heather, Kate and Erin had not solved their problem when they had? What if the problems kept on coming? What could I have done? It would have been time to nudge my students. There's nothing wrong with putting good ideas in people's heads. I would have said something like, "I have a feeling this class is just about ready to solve problems independently. I bet someone will surprise me soon with a solved inscription in the notebook. Boy, what a big day that would be!"

Much later, as I reflected on the abundance of problems in my classroom that fall, I made an interesting discovery. Other teachers who held class meetings complained that their class problems too reached a high peak a couple of months into the school year. It was almost as though the children surrendered their ability to solve problems in favor of being taken care of by the teacher. What was that about?

At the beginning of the school year children seem to come to us wearing a shield. They can't trust us yet. Then, as they develop a sense of safety, they can begin to allow their vulnerability to show, to expose their hurts and needs. However, at first children cannot modulate the expression of their needs. It's as though there is no valve to control the outpour. The dam breaks loose, and the discharge of feelings is uncontrollable.

When our notebook was bursting with problems, I had felt responsible. I had thought it was my fault that my students were helpless and socially incompetent, until, a few months later, when I saw a new resilience emerge, until my students started to take pride in solving their own problems, and began to modulate the flow between exposed vulnerability and coping strength.

Brave Enough to Tell the Truth

"Shireen was at my table. We were writing in our math journals. I was sitting when Shireen said, 'Shut up' to me. I said, 'Why did you do that?' But she didn't answer."

— Leo

Everyone liked Leo. A fair black boy with soft sandy curls crowning his head, he looked like a little lamb. At lunch he had the generosity to share his last potato chips, and at hockey congratulate the winning team, even when he was on the losing one.

Today Leo looked hurt and perplexed. He told us he'd been doing his work, minding his own business, when suddenly Shireen lashed out at him. He batted his long eyelashes to prevent the tears from rolling down his pudgy cheeks. He couldn't understand why she would have insulted him when he hadn't done anything wrong.

"Shireen, what happened?"

She spoke calmly and with dignity. "I didn't say shut up. He may have thought I said shut up, but I said, 'Shhh.'"

"Leo, tell us again what you heard Shireen say to you," I asked, needing to confirm the opposite stories in order to juxtapose the children's differing realities.

"I heard her say, 'Shut up.'"

"William, you were sitting at the same table, what did you hear?"

"I heard 'Shut up.'"

"Me, too," volunteered Tim who had been sitting at a neighboring table.

"Did anyone else hear what Shireen said?"

Silence.

"This must be difficult for Shireen. All our witnesses here say they heard the same thing. They heard her say, 'Shut up.'"

Shireen's body tightened.

"I know I said, 'Shhh,' 'cuz Leo and the others were being noisy, and that was bothering me!"

Leo's voice faltered. "I wasn't being noisy. I was just sitting down doing my work."

When I first started doing class meetings, I used to be the one who tried to name the problem. Today I was going to invite the children to name it for us.

"What's this problem about?"

"It's about saying, you know, bad words."

"It's about two kids having an argument."

"I think it's about not telling the truth."

"It's about disagreeing."

"I guess it's about feeling bad."

Leo's track record was impeccable. What about Shireen? Until now, I had been patient with her, listening, and giving her the benefit of the doubt, hoping that if she felt trusted and believed, she would no longer need to fabricate elaborate tales of victimization. Because she often muttered under her breath, it was difficult to catch her in the act, or confront her with the truth.

However, today my patience was failing me. Maybe I'd done her a disservice by believing her again and again. Maybe it gave her a false sense of reality, a sense that she could pull the wool over our eyes, that people, especially adults, weren't smart enough to see through her machinations.

I wanted Shireen to admit she had lied, but I didn't want her to feel coerced, because these methods of intimidation humiliate children. My role was not to break Shireen's spirit, but, instead, to engage her into being truthful.

Now was the time for a childhood story. "Children, let me tell you the story of the day I decided not to lie to my parents any more."

"I was eleven. One day my mom was napping, and I was doing my homework on the living-room coffee table instead of the kitchen table or my desk. I was copying some spelling words. I didn't realize how hard I was pressing with my pencil on the paper. So, what do you think happened?"

"You made marks on the table," said Ben.

"Yes, I was pressing so hard that my spelling words were getting engraved on my parents' expensive cherrywood table. I tried to rub them off with my hand, then with a cloth and some furniture polish. But nothing worked. So I decided not to say anything to my mother, hoping she wouldn't notice."

"You were scared she was gonna get mad at you?" asked Sofia.

"Yes. You see, I knew my mom would yell at me, so I kept my mouth shut. Well, of course, the next day my mother, who was a very sharp woman, noticed the ruined table top. She asked who had done it, and I felt my entire insides tremble with fear. I quickly thought maybe I could blame it on my little sister or my neighbor, Nora, who often did her homework with me. I didn't want to tell these lies, yet, at the same time, it was very scary to tell the truth. I knew my mom would have a fit. I didn't want to hear the screaming or face the punishment. Standing there in front of her felt like an eternity. Then I suddenly knew what I needed to do. I said, 'Mom, I did it. I'm sorry.'"

"What did she do?" exclaimed Erin horrified at the thought of getting into trouble, and being punished.

"Oh," I sighed, "she did had a fit. She screamed that I had ruined the table top, that it would cost a fortune to repair, that I was irresponsible. She went on and on, but I stood there like a brave tin soldier, scared on the inside, but very grown up on the outside. This was the first time I hadn't run away from the truth. And from that day on, I never lied to my parents."

"Did you get punished?" asked Ben with a hopeful gleam in his eyes. Fancy hearing that your teacher got punished as a child!

"Yes, I'm sure I did, but you know what? I don't even remember what it was. The memory that lasted over thirty years was telling the truth, not the punishment I got."

I looked at Shireen who was listening with visible pleasure and focused attention, and suddenly I remembered something brave and honest she had done, something that needed to be mentioned. Now.

"You know, Shireen, I remember how brave you were that day we were playing 'Medic Alert' out there on the field. Do you remember that?"

She nodded, barely able to contain the spreading grin on her face, exposing a gap in her gums where she had lost a tooth.

"Last week at sports Shireen accidentally hit someone on the head with her stuffed sock, so she came running to tell me what had happened, and to request her one-minute penalty. Now what do you think about that?"

"That was pretty brave," said Kate.

"Yeah, she wasn't afraid of getting the penalty," added Nina.

"She told the truth. She didn't say, 'I didn't do it'," said Tim.

All that time Shireen sat wide-eyed in disbelief. Never before had her classmates complemented her in public, and so unilaterally.

"Shireen, that day at sports you accepted your responsibility. You were honest with me. If you hold on to that memory, of the day you were honest and brave, you'll be able to do it again. I need you to be honest with me and everyone in our class. I will never get angry at you if you tell me the truth. You know me by now. I don't have fits, and go screaming around. Do I?"

The children giggled. But Shireen couldn't even smile. She sat silently with downcast eyes. She knew I wouldn't hurt her if she told the truth, but I wasn't sure she felt safe telling the truth at home.

"Think about it, when you tell the truth, people can trust you, they can count on you. When you say, 'I did it,' it's the bravest thing of all, even if the consequences are lousy, even if it's embarrassing and humiliating. I know you can do it."

Even though my words weren't harsh, I wondered whether I had been too judgmental of Shireen. Yet, giving her another chance, would have been accepting her lies, pretending she were innocent. I couldn't do that. It was time for her to take responsibility.

Perhaps Shireen was ready for a self-governing contract, but it was I who wasn't ready to administer one to her. Not yet. And I wasn't sure why.

I Don't Like Being Called a Racist

"Me, Heather, and Erin were playing in the dramatic corner. We were playing a game that was supposed to be realistic. Then Shireen started to play, and she played unrealistically. I told her not to play that way. It was not the kind of game we were playing. Then she got mad at me, and said that if she was white, she would be one of my best friends. Well, I am not racist against blacks. Me and Latoya are best friends, and a lot of other black people are my friends. Shireen also said that I was threatening her with the class notebook, but what I did, was just tell her that I was writing about her."

— Nina

Longest entry yet. Explosive material. As I read the entry at class meeting, I sensed tension mounting in the room. Or was it my own fears projected onto the children? I read in a serious, slow voice. On the surface, no affect whatsoever; on the inside, I was churning with anxiety.

"Nina, tell us what happened?"

Sitting sandwiched between Shireen and me, Nina began to speak in a calm and rational voice.

"I don't like being called a racist. It's really a strong word, you know." She paused, then turned to Shireen, "I wouldn't be your best friend, even if you were white, because of your attitude." Her voice climbed a decibel. "It's not the color of your skin, you know, it's your attitude."

"I didn't call you a racist!"

"Yes, you did. Do you think I would have been crying otherwise?" Then Nina turned to me. "Shireen said to me, 'I bet if I was white you'd be my best friend.'"

"No, I said, 'What is it? Is it my color?' because you forced me to be the baby, then the maid."

"I did not," shouted Nina, "you decided to be the maid."

"I couldn't be anything else. All the other kids in the dramatic corner were animals, and they were all acting crazy," argued Shireen.

I listened to the saga unfold, unable to respond or interrupt the heated discussion. It was plain to see, these two girls couldn't agree on anything.

"Then you threatened me," continued Shireen. "And you said, 'I'm going to write in the class notebook,' and you put the journal in my face."

Nina burst into tears. "No," she said between sobs, "I said...I said I was going to write in the notebook, because we're supposed to tell the other person when we're gonna use it. I...I didn't say it to threaten you."

"When Nina was writing in the notebook, I saw that she was actually crying," said William. Other children interrupted to agree with him. Then he continued. "But Nina didn't hold up the notebook to Shireen's face. I didn't see her do that."

"No, she did!" insisted Shireen.

"When I met Latoya," Nina said, "she told me you were a difficult person, but I tried to be your friend. But now I see that I wasn't meant to be your friend. I can't be your friend. You have a bad attitude. It won't get you anywhere in life. You won't have any friends."

Shireen covered her face with her hands, and cried out, "Everybody's mean to me! Everybody hates me!"

"Well, that's because you don't treat people fair!" yelled Nina.

The dialogue was hypnotic, like one of those riveting table tennis matches where the spectators' heads move swiftly from left to right in an attempt to keep track of the ball.

For the children's sake and mine, it was time to identify all the different layers of this problem.

"This is a hard meeting," I said, "I'm hearing several issues here: One, the issue of 'Can we be friends?' Two, 'Can we be friends regardless of the color of our skin?' Three, 'Who makes the decisions in the dramatic corner?' And four, 'Is it a threat when you tell someone you'll be writing in the notebook?'"

"Children, these are very hard questions. I'm sure Nina and Shireen are hurting a lot. You know, sometimes grown-ups struggle with similar issues—

issues of relationships, gender, race, power, laws. These are real problems in our world. So what can be done here in our class?"

It was crucial that we first discuss the hurt feelings concerning Nina and Shireen's friendship. The practical pieces about the dramatic corner or the use of the notebook, I was willing to defer to later.

"How can we help Nina and Shireen. Do you have any ideas?" I asked.

Shireen spoke first. "I think maybe we need a break from each other. We shouldn't play together for a while."

"We've done it before. It doesn't work," sighed Nina who pulled off her glasses to wipe her tear-stained face. "We always get into big fights when we take breaks."

I understood what Nina was saying. When they played separately, someone always felt left out, and cried. Because the classes at our school were relatively small, there was a limited number of potential friends. This all made it even harder when students needed a break from their usual playmates. To whom could they turn? In addition, because we stressed the importance of being inclusive while playing, our students might have felt at times pressured to accept playing with children with whom they didn't get along. Was that happening to Nina? Did she realize on an intuitive level that it was impossible to play with Shireen, and that at the same time there was no place to avoid her?

"My feelings get hurt when my friends' feelings are hurt," said Erin. "I think Nina can't be friends with Shireen, and Shireen can't be friends with Nina. That's all there is to it. They have different experiences. They just can't be friends."

Erin spoke with such assurance and conviction that she sounded like a politician delivering a speech. But what did she mean by "...They have different experiences?" Why should different life experiences be a bone of contention between two people?

As young as Erin was, she was on to something. Without knowing how to put it into words, she had an understanding that life experiences can sometimes divide people.

Last year Shireen and Latoya's relationship bristled from the start. I remember in the first weeks of school, overhearing Shireen at the art table saying to Latoya, "My mother's hair is nicer than your mother's hair." Shireen had made her remark in a singsongy voice, flashing a smug look on her face. Now Shireen stood on the outside, watching with envy, not comprehending her responsibility in what had happened, only feeling slighted and hurt. "Everybody hates me," was the way she could make sense of her experience. She couldn't hear Nina saying, "It's not the color of your skin. It's your attitude."

As I returned to our class meeting, I could tell Nina and Shireen's confrontation wasn't going to get resolved in one sitting.

"Children, it's time for lunch now. I know we're not finished, but sometimes it takes more than one meeting to resolve a problem. Hurt feelings take time to heal, and it takes time to listen, really listen to someone else."

After the children went off to lunch, I went to the staff room, and collapsed on the sofa to discuss what had transpired at the meeting. Even though I knew that waiting things out was often the answer, I still wanted to know how to make it better for Nina and Shireen. As I sat musing over their fate, and recounting to my colleagues what had happened at the meeting, I remembered an incident that had taken place two weeks earlier, and that helped me shed some light on Shireen's comments about racism.

Yvonne had had a day off from work, and had volunteered to help me with a messy and complicated art project in the classroom. After school she requested to talk to me because she was concerned that Shireen was being ostracized by the other girls. They were avoiding Shireen, she said, and excluding her from their jump-rope games. I reassured Yvonne that I'd look into the matter, talk with the girls and the yard supervising staff.

When I met with the girls, they denied any responsibility. "We include Shireen all the time," they argued, "but she always says we're not fair." The yard supervising staff was equally frustrated by the daily eruptions of angry feelings, but they hadn't witnessed any injustice done to Shireen.

Then one day after school I saw Yvonne dragging Shireen from the playground, and heading towards my classroom. She stood at my door in tears, clutching Shireen protectively under one arm.

"I'm not keeping my daughter here where she's not welcome," she managed to utter between sobs. "I'm taking her home right now."

Shireen remained silent, except for her deeply-set brown eyes that seemed to say, "See, my Mommy loves me. She's rescuing me."

I pleaded with Yvonne to wait, to talk with me, but to no avail. As she ran to the parking lot pulling Shireen by the arm, she cried out, "I can't talk now. We need to be with our family right now. I need to talk with my family."

And they took off.

I was left feeling inept and defeated. I knew nothing ever got resolved by running away, yet you can't force others to talk, and make peace when you're ready. They need to be ready, too.

Could Yvonne's interpretation of her daughter's exclusion in the playground as racial discrimination, have brought about Shireen's accusation of racism? Her questions mirrored her family's anger. Was "Is it my color?" a reflection of Yvonne's own experience of discrimination and rage?

After a couple of days of absence, Shireen came back to school. I didn't see Yvonne so I had no clue as to what had happened on the home front. I would have continued to speculate, had I not pursued her for some answers the same day of our class meeting.

When I addressed her, she seemed apathetic, which surprised me, since she tended to be chipper and full of smiles.

"Yvonne, can we talk?" I asked. "You were so hurt and angry the last time I saw you. How are things now?"

When I first began teaching, I didn't think of asking the black parents at our school why they had chosen a private school for their children. I didn't mention race in fear of offending someone, or displaying my ignorance. Now I have the courage to ask open and direct questions.

Yvonne told me she and her family were worried and angry about what was happening to Shireen in the playground. They thought the other girls were being racist toward her.

"I don't want my daughter to be treated that way by anyone," she said. Her hands were shaking, and her breath was halting. "Not by a white person, not by a black person, not by anyone."

"Yes, Yvonne," I'd responded. "I don't want any child in my care intimidated or bullied by anyone." I took a deep breath. "Yvonne, there might be some unhealthy dynamics happening at school between the girls. I don't think it's racial, but please give me a chance to observe for myself. I'll be out there all of next week at lunch. I'll gather some more information."

Yvonne's face relaxed. She was going to give me another chance.

Subtle Exclusions

My first day out in the yard—nothing unusual. I wasn't exactly tailing the girls, but I followed their activities from a reasonable distance without attracting their attention.

The next day something emerged. As the girls stood together trying to decide what to play, I noticed that Heather, Nina, Erin and Kate ended up forming a circle to discuss their game, while Shireen stood on the outside. How did that happen?

As the week wore on, I watched more closely. It happened again. As the girls were getting carried away discussing their plans, they started to turn their backs to Shireen until she was left to the side, on the outskirts of the circle and the decision-making process.

Shireen didn't seem to mind. Was she unaware of the subtleties of her classmates' body language? I was eager to jump in, but instead I watched for the consequences. After the girls had made their decisions, I noticed Shireen tended to be assigned roles that were more peripheral. "You get to be the guard," they'd say. "And the guard's house is over there." "Over there" was all the way across the playground. "You can be the kitten or the puppy, and your play area is over there." In both scenarios, Shireen's role forced her to play alone and at a distance of the central activity.

She did not always accept the decisions made for her. In fact, she often complained or sabotaged the game. The other girls would subsequently make accommodations to include her nearby. However, no one was satisfied, and things tended to quickly deteriorate into squabbles and injured feelings.

My week of playground observations had been informative. Now it was time to share it with the class. But how? And what would come of it?

At our next class meeting Sofia's notebook entry paved the way.

"Jessica said she would play with Shireen at lunch, too."

— Sofia

Sofia and Jessica had been an inseparable duo since kindergarten. They were known to play for extended periods of time in a kingdom they had created, imaginary-based and hermetically closed to others. It was always a game for two, and two only.

"Sofia, tell us about your entry," I asked at class meeting.

Shireen was absent that day. Usually when children involved in a notebook entry were absent, I waited for their return before dealing with the problem. However, today, the central issue appeared to have been between Jessica and Sofia and the management of their friendship. So, I decided to go ahead and discuss Sofia's entry.

"You see, Mona, it was like this," started Sofia who talked in an adult sort of way—confident and articulate. "Jessica told me that Shireen was going to play with us at recess. And that was okay with me. Then she told me Shireen was going to play with us at lunch, too." She placed a strong emphasis on "lunch, too," as though it was too much to swallow. Then she stopped, a little pout forming on her face.

"And how did that feel?"

"Not too good," she replied, her eyes downcast while busying herself flattening the pleats on her skirts.

"Did you let Jessica know about your feelings?"

"No, I guess not." She shrugged.

"Why not?"

"I...I...don't know."

I didn't want to press her.

"Jessica, what do you remember happened?"

"Mmm...it's not such a big deal, Sofia." Even with her speech impediment, Jessica never minced her words. She was known to be direct, very direct, so direct that sometimes her words stung. "I...mmm...I just let Shireen play with us. Mmm...that's all."

"Were you feeling a little jealous, Sofia?" asked Kate.

Eight months after having been introduced to class meetings, Kate was turning into a fine detective and facilitator.

It didn't surprise me when Sofia appeared uncomfortable. She was one of those overly responsible, adult-identified children who ardently desired to do the right thing. It was almost as though she were feeling guilty for being jealous.

"I'm not sure," started Sofia. "But I wanted to have some time alone with Jessica. I mean, everybody knows she's my best friend. I wanted to have time alone with her, that's all."

"Is it difficult when Shireen joins you?" I asked, realizing that the girls might be more at ease talking about Shireen in her absence.

"Yeah," said Sofia. "'Cuz when Shireen's with us, I don't get to play the games me and Jessica are used to playing. I mean it's different."

Erin added, "It's hard when Shireen plays with us, 'cuz she cries all the time when she can't get her way."

The opportunity was here. I had to say something. "Girls, I know Shireen is absent today, but I need to say this to you. What I'm going to say is hard, but necessary. There are certain subtle exclusions you do with Shireen that are not okay."

The girls looked startled.

"Remember, I was out in the playground last week, and I want to share my observations with you. I noticed you mean to include her in your games, but you give her mixed messages. You say, 'Yes, Shireen, you can play with us,' but then she's not included in the decision-making. You say, 'Yes, Shireen, you can be the guard, but your house is over there.' Did you notice that 'over there' is always across the playground, far away from where you play?"

Eyes widened around me. Hushed guilty silence pervading the room. I had uncovered what the girls weren't aware of, or thought was invisible. I remembered my own shame as a child when an adult found me out.

"A long time ago I used to be a little girl myself. I remember what I used to do with my best friends to protect our games. It's not that I would purposefully set out to do something harmful. I just wanted to have some power, but inevitably someone's feelings got hurt."

I wanted to have a dialogue with the girls, but instead it was turning into a monologue. Maybe I was being too zealous. Even though I was beginning to feel self-conscious, I went on.

"When I observed you at lunch, I saw you deciding on your games, and how Shireen was often left to the side while you turned your backs to her. You're probably not aware of it. It's a subtle body language. It contains no words, but it's communicated through your bodies. Here's an example."

"Let's pretend that Heather, here, was my best friend, and that I wanted to be alone with her." Heather was sitting next to me, so I turned around to face her. "Let's say I didn't want to share Heather with anyone. And I didn't want to say it to Lauren who was nearby, 'cause it's embarrassing and unkind to say, 'Sorry, but I don't want you around.' So I'll use my body to say it instead. I'll turn to face Heather, I'll get closer to her, and I'll turn my back to Lauren. Lauren, do you still feel like hanging around us under these circumstances?"

"No."

"What do you think my body is telling you?"

"Well, there's no room for me, it's like you're telling me to go away."

"And how does it feel?"

"Bad."

"Yes, I'd feel bad, too, if I were being rejected or excluded," I said. "So, do you see now how body language works? It is as hurtful as words. Do you think Shireen might experience feeling bad like Lauren did a moment ago in our simulation?"

"But Shireen starts all the fights...well, almost all of them, and then she cries all the time," whined Erin.

"Wouldn't you fight if there were some injustice done to you? Wouldn't you cry if you felt frustrated and rejected?"

Heavy silence. Everyone was uneasy, including me. This was the first time I was expressing such strong opinions at class meeting. I didn't have the patience for any more "benefits of the doubt." If I continued to neglect the girls' behavior, I'd be condoning it.

"Girls, when you play, you seem to give Shireen positions that have no power whatsoever, like the baby, the maid, the guard, the kitten, and then you place her at a distance. Do you think she's going to like it?"

"Well, no, I don't think she'd be very happy," said Nina with obvious remorse.

"I try to play with Shireen and be nice," said Kate. "But something always happens...I don't know how, but like...we'd be playing, let's say, and then she starts being mean, and then she cries, and everything falls apart."

"Yeah, I know," added Sofia. "It's not easy to play with her."

"You know, Sofia, you brought up an important problem. Today as we talked, we all realized that in a way when people get excluded, they lose their power. You didn't feel you had much power when Jessica invited Shireen to play. And that got us to talk about Shireen, and how she doesn't feel she has much power in our class, because she gets messages that make her feel left out. Now, let me ask, do you all think Shireen feels she has any power in general?"

"Oh, no!" cried Kate immediately. "I know she doesn't, because she always tells me that her grandpa is mean to her, and that her big brother hits her, and stuff like that."

"Yeah, I know," said Heather. "Sometimes she comes to school looking grumpy or sad, and she says that her baby brother was a pest, or that her grandpa yelled at her."

"I kind of feel sorry for her, 'cause she told me once that her grandpa loves Malcom more than her," said Kate.

"I guess it must be hard to feel unloved by an important grown-up in your life," I added. I decided to continue to discuss the world of sibling rivalry in order to include all the children in our discussion.

"Let me ask you something: Raise your hand if you have brothers or sisters, and feel that your parents love them more than they love you."

A number of hands went up. Maybe five. Those in the class who were only children were acting silly and raising their hands, too. Even though I had known that my class was primarily composed of older siblings and only children. I had never before realized the impact of birth order on my students' perceptions. If so many of my students were only children, could that explain how hard it was for them to hear someone else's viewpoint? And were so many students perfectionist and hard on themselves, because as older siblings they were adult-identified and driven to perform? Good questions to examine, but not now. I had more urgent issues to address.

"Now, raise your hand if you feel that your parents love you more than your brothers or sisters."

A smaller number of hands went up. Maybe three.

"Raise your hand if you feel that your parents are doing the best they can to love you and your siblings as equally as possible."

Most children raised their hand, even the ones who had already raised them before. They'd changed their mind. My last question had pushed them to acknowledge that, after all, their parents were doing the best possible job.

"You know, parents try to do their best, but they cannot love their children in the same way, because we are all so different. Let me tell you a story. When my middle son, Lex, was younger, he'd often ask me to tell him whom I loved the most of our three sons. Even though he knew my answer, 'cause it was always the same, he kept asking me to retell the story. I guess it must have reassured him. Well, I would tell him that I loved each one of them in a different way. I loved Jason, because he was my first child. He taught me what it was like to be a Mommy. He was my first teacher. It's always good to be in his company because he's calm and gentle. I loved Lex, because, of our three boys, he was the first to smile at me. He was barely a couple of weeks old, and he flashed me a great big smile. He always brought so much joy to my life with his jokes and his teasing. And as for Greg, he took a long time coming, because, well, maybe you've heard that sometimes it's not so easy to get pregnant or have a baby, that it takes some couples longer than they had thought, or they have health problems, well, this happened to me, and I had to be patient. So when Greg was finally born, you can imagine how happy I was, because he had been wanted for so long."

The children were listening, faces open with curiosity and anticipation.

"As parents, we try to be fair, but fairness doesn't mean giving exactly the same to every child. It means giving to each what each needs. Since we're all different individuals, and have different needs, we'll receive different gifts of love from our parents, grandparents, teachers, friends."

"And as a teacher, I try to give each and every one of you what it is that you need in order to learn and grow. Today the girls needed to hear about their subtle exclusions of Shireen, and how that may have affected their interactions. Next week Shireen will need to hear that some of her behaviors are not acceptable. Hopefully you will each learn and grow from these experiences."

By the end of the meeting I had made up my mind. Now that the girls' awareness had been raised, and now that I had called on their empathy to understand Shireen's position, I knew that I could help her with a self-governing contract. She was going to become socially accountable for her behavior in class. Pasong had started to benefit from his contract. He had been able to make friends, and keep them, and was included by the rest of the class. I wanted that to happen to Shireen, too. She deserved it.

That evening when I got home, I wondered why I had told my story about my sons. Did I sense that the girls needed some reassurance that I would continue to love them regardless of their failures and shortcomings, and that my love might take different forms depending on the situation?

How Could I Have Understood?

"Shireen," I addressed her at class meeting. 'You were absent last Friday, so I want to share with you what we discussed at the class meeting you missed."

She looked at me with caution, her eyebrows furrowed above her penetrating eyes as though to deflect any dangers that came hurling her way.

"Last week while I was observing kids playing outside, I noticed that you were often excluded from group discussions because of the way other kids huddled together to decide what to play. It didn't seem like they were deliberately turning their backs on you, but that kind of body language seemed to have excluded you from their activities."

All the time I was talking, my eyes were darting from Shireen to the girls involved—Kate, Heather, Nina, Erin, Jessica, Sofia. Shireen's face was circumspect. The others looked nervous. Heather, twirling a lock of her hair, occasionally chewing on the end of it. Erin biting her lower lip until it was scarlet. Kate and Nina's eyes cast down.

"Do you understand what I'm trying to say?" I asked in the heavy silence that enveloped the room.

"I don't know," she whispered.

"I know I would have been both hurt and angry if my friends had treated me that way," I suggested.

"Maybe now that we have talked about body language, you won't feel left out when kids are making decisions in the playground. You'll be able to choose which character you want to be, and you won't be asked to play far away from everyone." Then I addressed the rest of the class, "And I'm sure all the children in our class are going to become more aware of what their bodies are saying. It helps us all become more sensitive to each other."

"Shireen, I'm sorry. I bet you felt bad," said Kate. "See, we didn't know we were making you feel, you know, left out like that."

I could tell Shireen was overjoyed, but she couldn't indulge in that moment of recognition and apology, almost as though she were too afraid it might be retracted without notice.

Since she remained quiet, I spoke for her, allowing her a moment to compose herself. "Thank you for saying that, Kate. I'm sure Shireen appreciated hearing your words."

It was time to shift to our class notebook, and deal with yet another unresolved conflict involving Shireen. Even though the beginning of our meeting had been positive, and I didn't want to dampen everyone's spirits with the reality of what was to come, we had to move on. I read Nina's entry to the class.

> "Shireen was pushing the wagon. I was in it. It fell over. I fell down. After I stopped crying, Shireen asked me if I wanted to get back on. I said no. Then Shireen said, 'I see you think I did it on purpose.' I tried to talk to her, but she ignored me."
>
> — Nina

"Nina, tell us what happened."

There was pain in Nina's voice as she related the story. After telling us what happened, she added, "I know Shireen didn't do it on purpose. I mean, this wagon tips over all the time. But then, she ignored me when I tried to explain why I wouldn't get back in. She acted mad, and she walked away."

"How did you feeling when you fell off the wagon?"

"Well, I was scared. I didn't want to get back on. I was afraid it would happen again."

Even though Nina was a sturdy and stocky child, she lacked balance and physical coordination. Therefore, she was a bit on the cautious side when it came to physical activities. I imagined that falling off the wagon must have been disorienting and upsetting to her.

"Shireen, tell us what happened from your perspective?"

Shireen started with a soft, plaintive voice. Her story seemed to mirror Nina's, except for the last part. Shireen claimed that after the fall, she asked Nina to keep playing with her, not in the wagon, just playing, but that Nina had said she would never play with her again.

"That's not true!" shouted Nina, hurt and horrified by Shireen's rendition. "How can you say that? I never said that!"

"Girls, who's telling the truth?" I asked, trying to suppress the exasperation foaming up inside me. Wrong question, I knew it.

I didn't have to ask or speculate about the truth. I expected that even though the wagon tipping over was an accident, and that both girls knew it, Shireen must have felt responsible, and thus, uncomfortable. And when Nina refused to get back into the wagon, Shireen must have felt rejected and punished for the deed. So, what does a child like Shireen do when under duress? She becomes defensive to protect herself.

Shireen had always shown signs of being afraid of getting into trouble. One way she knew how to survive was to fabricate creative lies. I wonder how she perceived my flexibility and cooperation. Was I an understanding, patient teacher or a stupid sucker?

After considerable internal struggle, I took a risk, and let Shireen know that I saw through her game.

"Shireen, I'm wondering whether you couldn't hear what Nina had to say, because you felt responsible when she fell off the wagon. You heard that she didn't want to play with you forever, when, in fact, she just didn't want to get back into the wagon. Sometimes when I'm very upset about something, it's like I'm not really present. I'm so preoccupied that I don't hear what's being said to me."

Shireen looked puzzled at first, but then she recovered and argued,

"No. I heard Nina. I know she thought I did it on purpose."

Did Shireen understand what I was saying? Where did her combativeness come from? Perhaps when your reality gets knocked around by the people you love, you lose the ability to discern what's truly going on.

"I did not think you did it on purpose, Shireen!" interrupted Nina. "I tried to explain it to you, but you marched away. You always do that. You...you...don't let me explain things. You just get mad." Nina was getting flustered.

"Nina, since you didn't get a chance to explain things to Shireen after your fall, why don't you do it now?"

"Shireen," Nina said gently, but a bit impatiently, "I know the wagon is tippy. It was an accident. I don't blame you for it."

Shireen nodded with reluctance, and added, "But then, why didn't you want to play with me?" She sounded as though she were about to cry.

"I told you I was scared the wagon was going to tip over again, but it's like you didn't want to listen to me." Nina paused, then added, "If I had fallen off the wagon with Heather, she would have said, 'Are you all right?' A good friend helps you when you're sad or scared."

"Is that what you wished Shireen could have said to you?" I asked.

"Yeah."

Time to involve everyone in a class poll. "Children, what else can you do, when your friend is hurting? What do you do, or say when your friend is sad?"

The children were full of ideas which I was hoping could help Shireen.

"When my friend is crying, I get close to her and pat her on the back."

"If my friend gets hurt in the playground, like a cut or even a scratch, I call a teacher to help."

"I say, 'I'm sorry you're sad.' That kinda helps."

"Sometimes it's good to distract your friends when they're sad, like you can tell them a joke, or start a new game, or something."

"I don't know what to say to my friend when she's sad, but I just stay near her, or sit with her on one of the logs outside. I don't know, but I think it makes her feel better."

"These are great suggestions. Thank you. Maybe next time someone in our class is sad or hurting, you'll use some of these good ideas."

I knew it was time to talk to Shireen about the contract. It was like the necessary root canal appointment you dread, but can't avoid. Why was it so hard for me? I asked myself. Perhaps I feared that since Shireen was already feeling victimized, the contract would appear as yet another assault.

I turned to the class. "Children, how do you think Pasong's contract has helped him so far?"

An outburst of emotions. Cheering. Clapping.

"So what are you saying to me? That his behavior has improved?"

"Yeah, Pasong's not getting in as many fights."

"He doesn't tease me like he used to."

"I think it's really getting better. I mean Pasong is more patient when we play soccer."

"Pasong doesn't get as mad as before. You know, he used to get furious and stomp away when he didn't get his way. He doesn't do that any more."

The personal testimonies kept coming. I glanced at Pasong. He was turning his face left and right taking in all the compliments with pride and joy.

"Pasong, your classmates have noticed a difference in your behavior recently. What do you think?"

He pulled his shoulders back, and raised his head before speaking.

"Yeah, I'm better now," he said. "You know how before it was hard for me to control myself, well, now I think about how I could miss sports, and that helps me stop myself. Well, you know how I didn't like missing sports those two days, so I pay attention now."

"I'm happy for you. I can see the contract has helped you control your behavior. I can see how happy it makes you, and how happy your friends are."

"Shireen," I said. Her face turned to me, startled. "I want us to try a self-governing contract for you, too. We can all see how successful it has been for Pasong. Since I know how much you want to get along with your friends, why not try something special just for you, some logical consequence that can help you control yourself? What do you think?"

"Okay." It was hard to read her. The class was watching silently.

"Well, because I know sports is not one of your favorite activities, I don't think we should choose that, right?" I asked.

"Yeah." Her eyes looked frightened.

"How about art?" I said. "I know that's one of your favorite subjects."

"All right," she said. No expression on her face. Did she feel punished? Victimized? Did she experience relief? I couldn't tell.

I explained to her that if she were to behave in a way that hurt someone in our classroom, I would decide whether the contract would be activated. If it were, then the first time, she would miss one day of art, the second time, two days, and the third time, two weeks of art.

Just as I thought we were done, Kate raised her hand.

"Mona, I think that we should get a contract, too. This way it'll help us remember not to exclude Shireen with our body language. I mean, if she's going to try to use her self-control, I think we should, too."

Kate looked over in the direction of Heather, Erin, and Nina. Nina nodded with conviction. Heather and Erin seemed uncomfortable.

"I'm proud of you, Kate. You realized that you, too, had a responsibility in this matter. I'm sure that when everyone's working on the problem, it will improve." Turning to the other girls, I said, "What do you think?"

"I agree with Kate," said Nina. "It would help me remember to cooperate better with Shireen." Heather and Erin nodded in agreement.

Why didn't I think about a contract for Nina, Kate, Heather and Erin? I felt ashamed for not having thought of including the girls. It had been unfair to impose a contract on Shireen, and not consider one for those four girls. Maybe I thought at the time that contracts were more applicable to children who were out of control, someone like Shireen, or Pasong, for example, but not Nina, or Kate whose maturity and wisdom were well beyond their years. That was my prejudice.

The next day I approached Yvonne in the playground. The first thing I did was to agree with her that something had been amiss among the girls, and that Shireen had been, in fact, excluded from their games.

"But Yvonne, believe me, it wasn't racial."

Her face remained impenetrable, same face as her daughter.

"It's complicated the way people and relationships are, but I see two things," I continued. "One, the girls needed to hear how unkind their behavior toward Shireen had been. They had no idea how unfriendly they had been until I shared my observations with them. And two, Shireen needs to learn what it means to be a good friend, how to trust others and negotiate with them when conflicts arise. Do you know what I mean?"

Yes, she understood. Shireen had told her the content of our last class meeting, and Yvonne was pleased that the girls asked for a contract, too. There was some justice to this equation that appealed to her.

"I told Shireen she's got to mind her own business, and not get in trouble with those girls," said Yvonne. "But I don't know what it is with her, she's got to play with them, she says."

"They're her friends, that's why," I answered. "They mean a lot to her. I don't want Shireen, or any other student for that matter, to go about living life avoiding obstacles. Instead, I want them to learn how to tackle and overcome them. I'm sure all the children are learning lessons about getting along with people, and these lessons will serve them well throughout their lives."

Yvonne agreed.

I knew I hadn't undone the damage of the past two weeks, and as I drove home that evening I reluctantly realized I was naive to believe that all barriers could be overrun, and all problems overthrown.

I activated Shireen's contract only twice. Her behavior improved just as Pasong's had. But her attitude hadn't. She remained defensive, cautious, and brittle. Her contract had been successful only in curbing her conflicts with other children, but it had been unsuccessful in integrating her into the texture of the class, or in opening up new friendships.

The four girls faired well with their contracts, except for a couple of exclusion episodes. Kate and Nina, the more mature ones, made tremendous progress in taking Shireen into account in their decision-making, and in including her in their games. They were particularly aware of their body language.

Things were not altogether solved. Life didn't suddenly turn hunkydory. One thing I knew, there were fewer angry cries and accusations, misunderstandings, and tears. That was something.

• • •

Several years later, while I was doing errands in town, I ran into Yvonne.

"Hey, Mona, it's been so long!" she exclaimed with apparent pleasure at seeing me.

We embraced warmly as we stood in the rain on the front steps of the post office.

"How's Shireen doin'?" I asked eagerly. "I bet she's way taller than I am, but then of course, everybody is!"

She laughed. "Well, yes, she's big. We wear the same size clothes, if you can believe it!"

I nodded. "How's she doing in middle school?"

"She loves to read. That was a real gift you gave her—the love of books. But she still struggles with math."

She paused.

"You know, Shireen learned how to love learning when she was at your school. But as I look back on those years, I realize it wasn't the right place for us." With wet hair plastering her head, she sighed, pursed her lips, and said, "Every time Shireen went to play at someone's house, we came home feeling poorer than we were."

"I understand," is all I could say.

"I've got to run pick up Malcolm from school," she said as she waved at me, and disappeared in the parking lot.

It was arrogant to have said I understood. There was no way in a million years that I could have known what it felt like for her and for Shireen.

CHAPTER FIVE
Saying Goodbye

I Wish I Could Be in Third Grade Forever

End of May. Almost the end of the year. At our class meeting I ventured to say, "Hey, you guys! I'm out of business." I showed them the final empty page of the notebook. "Maybe I should go put an ad in the papers that says, 'Teacher out of work. Needs a class that can't get along together!'"

The children laughed. My usual teaching style tended to be more serious. But this day I had to be playful in order to balance off the slow creeping sadness, the sadness of the end of the year.

I chose to broach saying goodbye three weeks early in order to have enough time to discuss it again and again as the children discover new feelings inside them. At class meeting I read to the children my entry.

Dear Slippery Lizards,

I'm realizing that it's almost the end of the school year, and I'm getting sad.

I look forward to my summer vacation, but I'm also sad because in a few weeks we won't be a class anymore. You're all moving on to fourth grade, some of you here, others elsewhere. How are you feeling about all of this?

Love, Mona

The moment I had uttered those words, the reality of the end of the school year fell upon us. Of course, the past few weeks we had all anticipated it. Little things heralded the approaching summer, like the children wearing shorts and sandals again, the classroom windows and door open to create a draft, the long lines at the water fountain.

"Children, I always have such mixed feelings at the end of the school year. Do you know what I mean by mixed feelings?"

Jessica volunteered a definition. "It means being happy...mmm, and sad...at the same time."

"Yes, let's talk about the sadness first. I'm sad right now because the year is over. I'm going to miss you. I'll miss the community we have created this year."

Faces clouded. Slowly hands went up.

"I don't want to leave your classroom," said Kate.

"I know it's hard to leave behind the place you're familiar with, and the place you trust," I said.

Pasong was tentatively raising his hand. I needed to call on him quickly before he changed his mind.

"I don't want to get into trouble next year...I mean....I hope I'll make some friends...I hope the kids will like me."

I looked at him closely.

"You've grown so much this year that it's a little scary to fly off into the unknown. But, Pasong, what you've learned here, you'll be taking with you."

"But I can't take you with me," he blurted out.

"Well, not really take me with you, but in your heart you can. And you can always come visit me."

Silence enveloped the room.

Then Joseph spoke. "I remember when Pasong used to be in a lot of fights, like almost every day, but now it's different. He gets along with everybody."

Pasong's downcast eyes opened up again, and a tender smile spread across his face. Many children agreed with Joseph.

How wonderful that Joseph who, at the beginning of the year, was the first to write up a problem about Pasong in the class notebook, could end the year with such a compliment!

"You know, Pasong, when we change and grow, we never go back to the exact place we used to be. Sometimes we slip back into some of our bad habits for a while, but not for long, just long enough to adjust to the changes in our lives, and then we return to our new selves and continue to grow." I looked at him with questioning eyes. "Do you know what I mean?"

He nodded, but I knew it was all too scary for him. He had grown so much in the last few months, and was understandably afraid to lose what he had gained—the self-control, the respect of his friends, the stability at school.

Now I looked at Shireen. There was a blank look on her face. She and Jack weren't raising their hands. They sat quietly on the rug, listening to their friends. Were they feeling anxious? Or were they looking forward to leaving?

There were lots of hands in the air. I turned to Nina.

"I don't want to leave my friends," she said, her eyes shining with tears. "I know I'll still see them even when I'm in a different classroom, but it won't be the same."

"Yes, things can never be the same," I said. "And oftentimes that's what we miss the most in life, the same, the predictable. I also know how important your friends have been to you."

After we had exhausted all the possible reasons for being sad, I reminded my class that I had said I had mixed feelings.

"You know, children, I'm also very happy at the end of each school year. I'm happy, because you've learned and grown so much, and you've taught me a great deal, too. Every Friday at class meetings, you have shared a part of yourselves with me and with one another. I can't thank you enough."

The children were eager to share their happy feelings.

"I love summers, 'cause my family rents a cabin at the beach, and we have so much fun!"

"Even though I'm sad to leave all my friends, I'm kind of excited to make new ones."

"Every year after school's out, I can't wait for my birthday! It's in two weeks. This year it'll be a slumber party!"

"It's sort of fun to get to meet a new teacher."

"I'm excited about going to my older brother's school, 'cause they've got two big basketball courts in their playground, and I like to play basketball."

The children felt able to express their happiness about the future, because we had first taken the time to talk about what was hard. I heard their ambivalence, but I also heard their resiliency, their ability to dream, to hold on to something positive ahead. They were looking forward to life with hope and idealism.

The Following Week

On Monday morning the class was wild. I especially noticed Heather and Erin. They were defiant, disobedient, and arrogant. I'd never seen them act like that before. When I asked them to sit down and settle themselves, they looked at me with a smirk on their faces, thwarting authority the way a two-year-old laughs at a parent. They made loud annoying noises in class; they talked while I was giving instructions; they disturbed their table; they were rude to Tim. Other children followed suit.

I talked firmly about settling down to do our work.

"Children," I called out, feeling flushed and frustrated. "We have our Native American reports to finish in time before school ends. You need to stay focused on your work."

Then I pointed to our calendar. Together we counted the days left until school was out, 17, with in fact, only 15 days of school work, because we had two field trips coming up. The class was horrified. Was it a mistake to point out the reality to them? Perhaps it was wrong to shatter the illusion that we'd be together forever. Perhaps they needed their fantasy. After lunch the children continued to be terribly disruptive and disrespectful.

"Children, after we finish math we'll spend some of our Artist Workshop time having an emergency class meeting."

The word "emergency" shook them up. They sobered down a little.

During the meeting I asked, "I feel today is different for you, but I don't understand why. Tell me, if you can, what is different about today? Why is it difficult to use your self-control, to settle down and do your work, to respect each other and work together as a community?"

Many children wanted to talk. A few blamed it on their weekend.

"I had such a great time this weekend! It was sunny, so we went to the beach, and it felt so much like summer vacation, that I'm having a hard time being back at school," said Sofia.

"I had a lousy weekend," whined Nicko. "My mom wouldn't let me do something I wanted to do, so I'm in a bad mood today."

Then Kate offered a different interpretation.

"Maybe when you showed us on the calendar that there were only 17 more days of school, some kids thought they could be wild because school is almost out. It made them not care as much as before."

A number of children agreed with her. Nina added, "And it makes other kids feel, like, 'Well, if they're fooling around, why can't I?' and so more and more kids get wilder and wilder."

At the end of the meeting, Jack asked me, "Did you ever have an emergency class meeting with your other kids in your other class?"

"No, Jack, this is the first one."

I'm not sure why he asked. Did he feel bad about this meeting, or did he think our class was more special to me? Punishment or preferential treatment?

The last hour in the day went relatively well. The mood shifted to a lighter, more comfortable one. Maybe it was me. I had been experiencing chaos all day, a lack of control, a tumbling and stumbling feeling. Now I was at peace.

The next day I was detained five minutes after lunch due to a committee meeting, and when I entered my room, I saw the children sitting quietly at their tables. "You must be the best class in the whole world!" I complimented them.

The compliment didn't sit well with some of the children, and before I knew it, they spewed out that during my absence they had been terribly wild and noisy, standing on the tables and chairs. I listened calmly and asked if the children responsible would have the courage to raise their hands, without accusing anyone else. Nine children raised their hands, Pasong, Jack, Nicko, Jeremiah, Heather, Erin, Jessica and Sofia.

"Time for another emergency class meeting?" ventured Jack.

"Well, it looks like it, doesn't it?" I answered.

I asked if anyone was allowed to stand on tables at home. No one was, except for Lauren. She looked a bit worried when she realized her hand was the only one up. She quickly added, "I guess I'm a bit spoiled."

For a few minutes the children talked about what qualified as being spoiled. Then I reminded them that our classroom was like a home, that we spent more of our waking hours in our classroom than in our own homes, that our classroom deserved the same kind of respect.

The children agreed.

I went on to tell them I was sad to know that they still needed a parent, a teacher, or another adult to help them monitor their behavior.

"What about self-control, or what is sometimes called a conscience, that little voice inside you that tells you that something is right or wrong? Who hears this voice sometimes?"

All the children raised their hands. "Good," I said. "So what happened today? Where was that little voice?"

The children looked guilty and perplexed.

"We don't know how it happened," said Ben.

"Let me ask you something. Let's say you're in a candy store and you're really hungry and don't have any money. You want to steal a candy bar, but you don't. Did you not do it because you thought it was wrong to steal, or because you noticed a policeman in the next aisle?"

There was no hesitation. All the children said they wouldn't steal because they knew stealing was wrong whether there was a policeman or not.

"You know, climbing on the tables while I was out of the room is the same thing. It's not okay to do, whether I'm here or not."

I also brought up the issues of safety and hygiene. "I don't want anyone falling off a chair or table. It can be a dangerous fall, and your parents trust me to make our classroom a safe place for you."

When I started to tell them about stepping in cat poop in the sand outside, or in someone's spit, and then transferring it onto our tables on which we place our hands to do our work, I saw many disgusted faces. Volunteers quickly offered to sponge the tables clean.

I was curious about how the children were internalizing this incident, so I asked, "I know you won't do anything like this again in our classroom while I'm gone, so would you like us to go on to math, and forget all about what happened today? Or would you prefer we talk about a possible punishment?"

Unanimously and without any hesitation, the children wanted to talk about punishments. I asked for suggestions. "I won't accept jail sentences," I joked to lighten the mood. They laughed.

They came up with three ideas for punishments—missing part of one lunch recess, missing part of one free choice time, missing part of a favorite subject, such as silent reading, or drawing during chapter book.

I asked them to close their eyes, and put their heads down on the tables for a genuine vote without the influence of friends. The majority voted for missing part of one lunch recess.

Only Jack complained a bit. He didn't want to miss playing baseball at lunch, but he reluctantly agreed.

"Do you think this punishment should be fun, or does it have to hurt a little bit?" I asked.

"It's got to hurt, so that you don't do it again," said Nicko. "This way next time you think about what'll happen and it makes you stop." He seemed full of experience. Sometimes children can be preachy as they mimic their parents' admonitions.

It was time to move on to our fraction unit in math.

I asked the class, "How do you feel now?"

"Good," was the resounding response. I could almost see relief and pleasure on the children's faces. Retribution alleviated their guilt.

At our last class meeting of the year, I surprised the children with an entry.

Dear Slippery Lizards,

Last week we talked about saying goodbye at the end of the year, and how sad it makes us feel. I've also noticed that this week you were wilder than usual. I have an idea what that might be about. Let's talk about it.

Love, Mona

The children listened attentively as I gave them my interpretation of what had happened this week for our class.

"You know children, when I was in fourth grade, I just loved my teacher and my class. We loved that year so much that we didn't want it to end. But as it was nearing the end, we started to act out, and be wild in the classroom. We got our teacher, Sister Magdalena, so mad that she began yelling at us all the time. We didn't know why we were being disruptive and disrespectful. Slowly it became easier to say to ourselves, 'Hey, we don't like this Sister Magdalena anymore, she yells too much. We're glad we're going on to fifth grade. Who wants to be in her class anyway?"

The children were mesmerized by my tale. "Does anyone think that perhaps this week you were feeling the same way I was feeling in fourth grade?" I asked.

"I agree with your story," said Kate in a serious tone of voice. "I think we were wild this week, 'cause we wanted to pretend it didn't matter to leave our class."

Others offered similar views.

"It's hard to go on to another classroom."

"I love my friends here."

"I wish I could be in third grade forever."

Heather who was never disruptive, and who had been one of the most disruptive on Monday, shared with us that on Friday, after we had talked about the end of the school year, she went home and cried and cried for a long time.

She started to cry again. Nina's eyes were brimming with tears. I felt my own tears starting to well up, too. "You know, Heather, I, too, have been sad a lot lately. I cried, too, last night thinking about how hard it is to say goodbye to all of you. You've been the greatest class, the wisest, and the best!"

I didn't know why, but I started to tell them how when I was a child I lost my home. Perhaps I felt it was the last chance I had to share my story with them. I told them how at the end of fourth grade I lost my home in Egypt, my relatives, my nanny, my toys, and my best friend, Therese. My parents and sister were with me, and together we became political refugees with only two suitcases to our name.

Some children asked me questions, others expressed sympathy for my plight, but what seemed to fascinate them the most was the loss of my nanny. It led them to tell their own stories of lost baby-sitters, the ones they missed, the ones they had truly loved. I wondered if they had chosen this metaphor to talk about losing me and the year we had created together.

When suddenly Kate, who had been unusually quiet and deep in thought, took me by surprise. "Mona, your nanny was like your mother, but not your mother."

"That's like my adopted mom," interrupted Pasong. "She's my mom, but not my mom."

Pasong, the boy who at the beginning of the year never seemed to know why, now had the words to say it. What is, but isn't, what was, but wasn't—that's what it was all about, that's what we had spent the whole year discussing—the tension between what is visible on the outside, and what is hidden on the inside, the conflict between our individual reality, and the realities of others.

"Yeah," I said nodding slowly, unable to add anything.

There was nothing to add, nothing to clarify, or embellish. It was time to say good-bye.

Postscript For Teachers: The Nuts and Bolts

4. What do you do when the problem written up in the notebook involves a student from a different class, or an adult at the school?
5. What if the problem written up in the notebook is a private family matter, or a matter that doesn't pertain to school life?
6. What do you do when a problem keeps coming up over and over?
7. What about the squirmy child who can't sit still during class meeting?
8. What do you do about the quiet child who doesn't participate during the class meeting?
9. What about the child who monopolizes the meeting?
10. What is the ideal group size for class meetings?
11. Have you done class meetings with different ethnic or socioeconomic communities than your own?
12. For what age levels are class meetings best suited?
13. What about students in middle school or high school?
14. What mechanism do you use to keep an individual child from feeling scapegoated or picked on by the group?
15. Do you allow observers during class meetings?
16. What do you do when students use the notebook to threaten their classmates or tattle on them?
17. Can anyone do class meetings? How much training, if any, does one need to conduct them?

Introduction

Since my book is a collection of stories about my classroom that illustrate how class meetings helped the children develop empathy and create a sense of community, I thought it would be useful to include specific information about the how-tos of class meetings. When I offer workshops on class meetings I am always impressed by the thoughtful questions teachers ask me. Their questions help me reflect and fine tune my own model. Therefore, in this Postscript, I will attempt to give concrete guidance and support to the teachers interested in establishing class meetings in their classrooms.

It isn't easy to facilitate class meetings. It takes patience and skill. For one thing, there is no formula you can universally apply to every problem. Just as life is full of complexities, contradictions, exceptions—all the things we cannot control—classrooms abound in them. As a teacher I might feel that I exert some control when I hand out the weekly spelling list, or teach the multiplication tables. However, doing class meetings is another story, because engaging children in conversation deals with the unpredictable realm of emotions.

Nevertheless, I learned how to provide my students with a weekly structure that helped them develop strategies for life. The dialogues we had throughout the year challenged our notions of group life and changed us all. We started off in September as separate individuals, some connected by friendship, others loners on the periphery of the group. By the end of the year we had learned how to live with one another and how to tolerate each other's idiosyncrasies. We had developed values to live by, even though we still experienced, like any other community in the world, a fair share of strife and conflict. However, the difference lay in the fact that we had created a space where once a week we talked about the hard things, we listened to one another with respect, consoled a sad friend, supported a needy one, confronted a bully, or rejoiced in each other's progress.

In this Postscript, I try to dissect class meetings, and the process you read about in my stories. I give you step by step instructions, and I answer the questions most frequently asked by teachers at class meeting workshops. I hope you will experiment with my model and create your own process and intimate climate using the tools I have developed—while integrating your own students and who you are as a teacher, your style, degree of comfort, and personality.

Learning to do class meetings involves making mistakes, falling down, and getting back up again. Don't get discouraged. With time and experience you'll find out that it's well worth it.

How Class Meetings Came About

Disruptive Behaviors in the Classroom Leading to Class Meetings

Eight years ago I became very frustrated with the daily conflicts in my classroom. I was teaching a second-third grade combination with a challenging group of children, unable to negotiate, or resolve their own conflicts. There were constant emotional eruptions and tears. In short, it seemed as though the children spent the entire day reacting to one another.

The make-up of my class was not unlike many of the classrooms in California. Many of my students had special needs—learning and/or social and emotional needs. Some of the needs had been already identified by previous teachers, and these students were getting special assistance, while other needs had gone undetected, and I was in the process of making referrals to the parents for evaluations. These are the most obvious behaviors that were manifested daily in my classroom:

Impulsivity, both Verbal and Physical The children often blurted out in class. Not only did they not raise their hands to talk, but they also didn't know how to take turns, or listen to one another. When sitting on the rug for a story or discussion, or while walking down the halls, the children chanted, jostled, touched and pushed one another, not aware of each other's physical boundaries, as though they couldn't anticipate where they ended and someone else began.

Distractibility Many of my students had attentional difficulties. They couldn't remain focused on their work. Any small noise or disruption interrupted their concentration.

Difficulty Beginning Independent Projects The children had a hard time when expected to work on projects that required organization. That's when many of them invariably chose to amble off to the bathroom, or to sharpen their pencils. Some children used silliness and clowning behaviors to get the attention of their classmates in order to avoid challenging work. Of course, all of these disruptions broke the concentration of the few focused students remaining at the tables, making the completion of their projects an impossible task.

Difficulty with Transitions One of the most surprising things was that, even though many of my students were unable to focus during independent work time, they could easily become hyperfocused during other activities such as silent reading or art, which made it challenging to disengage them from their concentration. And because it had been such a feat to settle them into one activity, I often dreaded the inevitable interruptions and transitions, such as going to recess, lunch, or to an enrichment teacher. It had taken so much of my energy to get them all calmed down and settled, that I didn't dare break the spell. When I finally did get their attention to transition, it seemed as though a tornado hit our classroom as everyone flew in every direction, putting materials away, pushing chairs in, picking up folders strewn on the floor, all the time while pushing, chanting, running. It was pure mayhem.

Difficulty Processing Information I found myself having to repeat instructions all the time. The children appeared attentive, yet as I explained a multiple-step task, I could see from the confused look on their faces that I had lost them after step one. To help them follow my oral directions better, I began writing them on the board, so the children could refer to them as they went along doing their work.

Character and Community in the Classroom

Needless to say, I felt totally overwhelmed with the behaviors I saw in my classroom. It distressed me that so many of my students couldn't focus and listen to one another. The children were very sweet and eager to learn, yet their self-esteem was low. How was I going to create class community when many of these children couldn't even see beyond themselves? And how was I going to teach reading, writing and math, if I was spending my days putting out one fire after another. I was worried that this group of children was going to compromise my academic curriculum, and my goal of helping them develop into empathic human beings.

Because I believe that teaching is a process of inquiry, and because I see myself as a teacher-researcher, I stopped and formulated some questions and goals for myself. In addition, I discussed my observations and frustrations with my director who became an important part of my research and reflection.

- How can I provide all of my students with a safe classroom that enables them to learn?
- How can I provide them with an intellectual environment if the learning is constantly interrupted?
- How can I create an empathic and supportive class community if there is so much conflict?
- How do I help the marginalized student, the peripheral child with the bad reputation, fit in?

Researching Existing Class Meeting Models

I set out to do my own research. The summer following this challenging group of students, I started to read books in the field of conflict resolution. I read *Tribes*, the works of William Glasser, and Jane Nelson's class meeting model. I became interested in the work of Dr. Francoise Dolto, a French pediatrician and psychoanalyst, who wrote about consulting for an alternative school in Normandy. I was especially impressed with Dr. Dolto's attempts at helping children with special needs become better integrated in the school system.

Most models I read about depicted weekly class meetings when everyone comes together to discuss the conflicts and issues of the week, and to make management decisions together. Some of the models were more formulaic than others. I chose to adapt Dr. Francoise Dolto's model, because it resonated with my precepts and my own personal style of teaching. I wanted my students to experience self-determination and to share the power of daily classroom management. I also wanted to create a class community where the children experienced a sense of belonging, where they felt connected, and where they were encouraged to care about one another.

So the following fall, with the knowledge that developmentally my students were beginning to listen to one another, and take someone else's viewpoint, I instituted my own class meetings.

Class Meeting Format—The Logistics

Every year in the first week of school, I gather my students in our book corner, which is a cozy spot covered with a nice thick rug. We sit in a circle so that we can see each other's faces, and I tell the children that every week we will meet as a group to discuss how well we are getting along, what is working and what's not working, and how to solve our own problems. Then I explain the different components of class meetings.

Regularity

I tell the children that every Friday morning before lunch we will meet on this rug to discuss how well we're getting along. At the beginning of the year I start with meetings of 20 to 30 minutes, but by the end of the year, as the children develop the patience and maturity to sit for a longer period, our meetings last 40 to 45 minutes. I tell the children that we will meet every week, because class meetings are just as important as math, writing, reading, or science.

Class Notebook, Pencil, and Hourglass

I show the children a basket in which I've placed a blank notebook labeled "Class Meetings" and the dates of our academic school year. The basket also contains a nice pencil (something more fanciful than what we use every day), and a whimsical water hour glass—the kind that has colorful water running through a spinning wheel. I use the hour glass for a minute of silence at the beginning of each class meeting to help us transition to a different level of social and emotional communication, and to help us reflect on how we're doing as a community. The colorful water provides a focal point for the children who are thus able to be quiet and serious.

Structuring the Notebook, Facilitating the Meeting

I explain to the children that if they have a problem at school with one of their classmates, or anyone else (students or teachers from other classrooms), they can write their problems in the class notebook. Here is how they need to do it:

1. *They write down the date.*

   I request the date because I like to document the events that take place in our school year. It's the teacher-researcher instinct in me.

2. *They write down their entry with just enough information so we can figure out what the problem is about.*

   It shouldn't be a detailed account since they'll get a chance to explain more fully at the meeting. They must write the names of the people with whom they're having problems. Children often begin telling about a problem with this disclaimer: "I don't want to mention any names, but this person in our class..." They have been trained not to embarrass someone publicly, however, by using vague and amorphous comments, we create a community filled with secrecy and covert accusations. Therefore, I ask that the children not be afraid of being direct. I encourage them to speak their minds with honesty, but also with respect. Another reason is that I want children who have been troublesome to be mentioned by name. I don't want them to hide and keep on doing what they're doing because no one has asked them directly to take responsibility for their actions. It's important that everyone in our class be seen and heard if we are to expect people to change, and become part of a community.

3. *They must sign their name after their entry.*

   By signing their name at the end of their entries, children show that they have the courage to express their grievances in a public forum. I don't want anonymous accusations to start filling up the notebook, and destroying the trust I'm trying to create. Community cannot be built on secrets and anonymity.

4. *They turn the page over and place a large metal clip to mark the page.*

   By turning the page and using a clip, we give the writer of the previous entry a little bit of privacy so the next person writing in the notebook doesn't read the preceding entry. Of course, the clip doesn't guarantee real privacy. A student interested in reading a previous entry can always pull off the clip and read the previous pages. However, that has not been a problem. The clip's place becomes a sacred thing for the children.

5. *Before writing down a problem, the student must first attempt to solve it.*

I don't want class meetings to become a crutch for the children, or a place to tattle on each other. Therefore, it's important they know that their initiative to resolve their own conflicts is encouraged, and that they must first try to solve their own problems before writing them up in the notebook. I tell the children, "Ask the other child, 'Do you want to solve our problem?' If the child doesn't agree to talk it over, you can respond by saying, 'Then I'll have to write it up in the notebook so our class can help us at our next class meeting.'" This gentle reminder will often prompt a reluctant compromiser to make peace, but it will also forewarn the stubborn child that this issue will be discussed publicly. It's important the children not be surprised or embarrassed to hear their names mentioned at class meeting.

6. *If students solve a problem after it's been written up, but before the next class meeting takes place, they can write a big "S" over the written problem to signify that it's been solved.*

I don't want problems erased from the notebook, or pages torn out when children solve their problems before our meetings. The reasons I want the problems to remain in our notebook, are: one, I'd like to have all the problems of the year documented, and, two, I'd like to publicly recognize and praise the students who have been successful at solving their own problems outside of our meetings. By weaning the needy children who use the notebook to get attention, I help empower them so that they get our attention for being independent and resourceful.

7. *The structure of the meetings is reliable and consistent.*

I tell the children that this is not a court of justice. I'm not a judge who will take sides. I'm here to help them talk and listen to one another. I explain how the meetings are run. First a minute of silence to think back on our week, and consider how well we've been getting along together. Then I read the first entry in the notebook. The child who has written it, explains more fully what's happened. The other child who has been written about, listens and waits for his or her turn. During the children's explanations, I listen carefully, and remain impartial. Sometimes I ask a question, or ask the child how he or she was feeling at the time.

After both children have had a chance to explain their respective perspectives, I turn to the class and involve the rest of the children by asking them if they've experienced a similar problem, and if so, how they resolved it. Some children tell us their stories, others tell us they've witnessed the problem at hand. As we move our focus away from the two protagonists, we discuss what the problem is about, and how it might be resolved. The children begin to share examples from their lives, their hurts, their joys, their successes and defeats. It is in this slow, spontaneous and unselfconscious unveiling that we begin to truly care about one another. This dialogue helps forge our ties, and commits us to one another. This is how our community is created.

Here is a short example that clearly demonstrates the power of change. One day at a class meeting Sophia told us that Jeremiah, her math partner, had taken over the math activity, and hadn't let her do very much. However, Jeremiah claimed he hadn't been bossy.

Two days later, when Sophia and Jeremiah were partnered up again for math, I saw Jeremiah control most of the activity. At the end of math, as we debriefed, Sophia expressed again her frustration in working with Jeremiah.

I turned to Jeremiah and asked him if he felt the power had been shared equally between the two of them.

Surprised by my question, Jeremiah looked down, and shook his head, but an instant later, he raised it, cocked it to one side, and said in a musing tone of voice, "But you know, it wasn't that bad. I mean...it was like 40/60."

Oh, he recognizes his power, I thought.

Then he continued, "You know, it's not like I had 100%, and she had 0%."

Without missing a beat, Sophia retorted, "Well, I think it was more like 20/80."

"Sophia, what would you like it to be?" I asked.

"50/50," she said.

I looked at Jeremiah. With cheeks flushing, he agreed.

The next day, following math, when I asked Sophia how things had gone, she said smiling, "It was 49/51, but that's okay."

We all knew that Jeremiah had had the slight advantage, but it seemed all right with Sophia. She was empowered and happy, and Jeremiah was beginning to share his power.

Emotions are slow learners, but this is how Jeremiah learned about other people's perspectives. By putting this whole concept into numbers—something Jeremiah understood very well—he was slowly able to see Sophia's viewpoint and begin to change. Sophia, on the other hand, was given the support she needed to express her grievances, and stand up to Jeremiah.

Interestingly, since Jeremiah and Sophia's conflict, our class has had good conversations about sharing the power in the classroom. Many children in the class have chosen to adopt the "percentage method" to negotiate their power struggles. I will often hear one child say to another, "Wait a minute, that's not fair, it feels like 30/70!"

Confronted with someone else's reality, children can begin to change their perspectives and behaviors while taking into consideration other people's feelings and opinions.

The Self-Governing Contract

Class meetings work for most children. But how about the children for whom class meetings are not enough? Every classroom has a number of them for whom change is painstakingly slow, and often frustrating. These children are either more rigid temperamentally, impulsive by nature, or are not able to cope with larger familial issues that spill into the classroom. Since these children cannot internalize self-control, it is crucial that we give them the tools with which to practice in order to experience a sense of success at growing up and being part of the class community.

Because I'm not a teacher who relies on behaviorist methods in the classroom, I had a hard time appreciating that, without some form of external control, these children who were failing at getting along with others were becoming more and more disenfranchised and marginalized. Since I accommodated for my students with special cognitive needs in the classroom, I realized that I needed to become more flexible as a teacher, and accommodate for the needs of my special social cases. This is how self-governing contracts came about.

At the beginning of the year I introduce the self-governing contract to my class. We first try to define it. What does "governing" mean? Why is it called "self-governing?" What is a contract? Then I tell them about it.

"It's a tool that can help you change a behavior you don't like about yourself. Some kids are constantly late to school. They don't like it; it embarrasses them. They want to change. A contract is good for that. Other kids don't bring in their homework on time. A contract will help them become more responsible. Some kids annoy others, and that's not a good thing if you want to make friends. A contract will help them, too."

I tell the children that I usually don't impose the contract on my students, but that instead, I prefer that they, themselves, come to the realization that their behavior would benefit from some kind of control. However, if they can't make that decision themselves, I might have to encourage them, and in some rare cases, impose the contract myself.

The next important thing to explain, is that a contract is not a punishment. It's an agreement between the child and the community which includes classmates, teachers and parents. And that we, the community, will help support the child who wants to make a positive change because it's very hard to change alone. I go on to tell them that grown-ups who can't stop smoking, or who would like to lose weight, or who would like to exercise regularly, will often join a group that will help support them while they're trying to change and use their self-control. It's important children hear that they're not alone in trying to make changes, and that adults, too, make attempts at changing their behavior. Then I explain the terms of the contract:

"If you want to improve your behavior, or try to change something you don't like about yourself, you need to come talk to me, or write it up in the class notebook. If I notice that you might need a contract, but you're not bringing it up to me, I'll need to encourage you to do it.

"Next, you'll have to choose an activity you love to do in class which you'd be willing to give up if you break your contract."

I explain that it can be anything except recess, since I want them to have their daily exercise and free play. However, it can be anything else they look forward to during school time. Often the children choose silent reading, drawing during chapter book, or playing math board games. All these activities are part of our daily schedule, and last about 20 minutes. (A sample of a blank contract appears on page 131.)

Self-Governing Contract

A self-governing contract is a mechanism of social control for enforcing our classroom community standards. It is an official agreement that supports a child who has decided to make a positive behavioral change. This contract is put into action only after other attempts to make positive change have failed. With the contract, the child agrees to give up a favorite school activity if the negative behavior occurs. Knowing there will be a specific and undesirable consequence will help the child decide to choose an appropriate prosocial behavior.

_____ has chosen to give up:

<small>Print child's name</small>

_____ if these negative actions occur:

<small>Print name of activity</small>

_____.

The contract is as follows:

1st offense: _____ missses one day of the chosen activity.

2nd offense: _____ misses two days.

3rd offense: _____ misses a whole week.

After the 3rd offense, we start back at the 1st offense.

_____   _____

<small>Student signature</small>   <small>Parent signature</small>

_____   _____

<small>Teacher signature</small>   <small>Date</small>

Classmates' signatures:

_____

_____

_____

After the student and I sign and date the contract, the rest of the class gets to sign the contract, too. It is often endearing to read the comments of encouragement the children write next to their signatures—"Go Pasong!" "You can do it, Shireen!" Everyone is invested in seeing the child on the contract be successful.

I remember how one child, Rachel, called Eleanore every Thursday night in order to remind her to bring in her homework folder on Friday morning. Rachel wanted to be a supportive friend to Eleanore. Other children support the child on a contract by congratulating, encouraging, reminding, forgiving, and mostly by being a good friend.

Then the child takes the contract home for the parents to sign. Often parents are grateful that the whole class is helping their child in becoming more self-controlled and responsible. They also want to see their child become better integrated in the social scene at school, making friends, and getting positive feedback for positive behaviors.

The contract is then returned to school, where, upon the children's request, I post it on one of our classroom bulletin boards for the world to see. The children are not ashamed of their contracts, on the contrary, they're the ones who request such exposure, and are very proud of their effort at changing, and of their classmates' enthusiastic and unequivocal support.

I tell the class, "If you can't control yourself, I'm the one, in discussion with you, who decides if this is an offense that warrants activating the contract or not. I don't want other children to hold that power over you." The children are grateful that their classmates won't try to get them in trouble which would have actually defeated our efforts at working together.

Very quickly the children realize that being denied a favorite activity hurts a little bit. The first time Jamal broke his contract, he had to give up one day of silent reading. It was hard for him since he just adored reading. When everyone settled on the rug to read, Jamal sat on a nearby chair, and watched the other children pouring over their books. Later that day, he told me that he was going to try really hard to stay at step one of the contract, because he couldn't bear going through the torture of missing reading again, and having to watch his friends read. It was just too hard to do.

As I reflect on the role of the self-governing contract for our class, I realize that Jamal and the other children who couldn't show improvement or change as a result of our discussions at class meetings, made real progress after taking on a self-governing contract. For these children, the external control and support made the difference. Now they could experience feeling successful, and seeing how much their classmates cared for them and supported them. They became more connected to all of us as valued members of our community.

The Roles of Mirror, Scribe, and Historian

One of the reasons I remained devoted to doing class meetings, even when times were difficult, was that I had the opportunity to work with Jill Alban, a learning specialist and colleague who had become my mirror and scribe. Jill and I first met when she came into my classroom to work with some of the children who had special needs. She became interested in observing how her students made use of the class meetings, how attentive they were, and how they expressed themselves verbally. She was also interested in witnessing the class meeting process.

Originally, I hadn't planned on having another professional observe my meetings. What started out as Jill's interest in her students and in class meetings, slowly became for the two of us a work of collaboration and reflection. Over the past years Jill, with pad and pencil in hand, sat on the edge of our circle, taking notes, and later helping me debrief and reflect about the meetings. She listened carefully when I was concerned about one of my students, when I felt unsure about the way I had responded to a child, or when I experienced frustration, and wanted to give up.

Even after only one year of class meetings, it became clear that Jill's role had become crucial to the success of our class community. I couldn't have mustered the courage and perseverance in the face of our weekly hurdles, had it not been for Jill's unconditional support, her keen observations of the children, and her ability to discern the major themes that arose throughout the year.

Because teaching is an isolating profession, it's important that two teachers work together in order to maintain the courage to do the meetings, and develop the insights that give meaning to working with children. Ideally, every teacher doing class meetings needs to pair up with another professional who can observe the process, and reflect on it later.

In addition to being my mirror and scribe, Jill became my historian. Because she could observe the meetings, and not be as affected by the children's emotions, she had the privileged position of seeing the social patterns and themes that slowly evolved in our class.

When Jill and I looked back on that first year, we recognized two stages of class meetings. Stage one was characterized by a multitude of problems written in the notebook—small petty grievances that are often perceived by teachers as the nuisances and trademark of childhood: "He pushed me," "She teased me," "He took my pencil," "She laughed at me," etc. Some of the more vulnerable children seemed to write weekly about their difficulties getting along with others in the classroom and on the playground. Some children began to use the notebook as a way of threatening their classmates: "If you keep bothering me, I'm going to write you up in the notebook." The threats and misuse of the notebook were discussed during class meetings. The children were encouraged to solve their own problems, and praised for not using the class meetings to resolve problems they could manage on their own.

By the middle of the school year, many children were solving their problems independently. We also saw a shift occur in the kinds of issues written in the notebook. Stage two was characterized by problems that were signed by several children. We noted that instead of problems written by one child about another child, the conflicts appeared to be between a number of children, and began to uncover important issues. The small petty grievances of September and October were replaced by larger themes.

The boys often wrote about sports, rules, sportsmanship, while the girls' problems were mostly about relationships, friendship, and issues that pertained to feeling included or excluded. One of the central themes that encompassed both genders had to do, not surprisingly, with power and popularity in the classroom and on the playground.

As our historian and scribe, Jill helped me articulate not only the themes of class meetings, but also the growth we saw occurring among the children.

- They were learning how to resolve their conflicts independently.
- They were making friends.
- They were listening to one another, and controlling their behavior.
- They were more appreciative of one another's perspectives.

- They were learning how to distinguish between a big problem that needed everyone's attention, and a minor spat that could be overlooked.
- They began talking about issues that pertained to important social problems, such as racism, sexism, ageism, homophobia, classism, etc.
- Finally, they were learning how to live and work together as a community.

Questions and Answers

When I offer a workshop on class meetings for teachers, I often get asked very interesting questions about the logistics of my work. In this section I have compiled the questions most often asked by teachers in the hopes that they will be useful to the reader interested in starting class meetings.

Question:

How do you get to all of the problems during class meeting?

Answer:

I try to spend about fifteen minutes per problem. The night before the class meeting, I open our class notebook to check how many problems are in the book. If there are more than three, I often prioritize them in my mind, so I can get to the important ones first in case we run out of time. The next day I ask the children to prioritize them by degree of importance. It's always interesting to me to see who can wait, and who can't. I also read them to myself ahead of time to see if there are common threads that run through them, such as issues of teasing, or name calling. If I see problems that deal with similar issues, I lump them together for matters of expediency. The next day at the meeting I read the problems to the children, and ask them to guess why I put those problems together. Often the children are savvy enough to see the similarities.

One year I had a class that didn't tolerate the small vicissitudes of life. Everything seemed to annoy everyone. The day I counted 21 problems, I knew it was time to discuss what makes for a small problem you solve on your own, and what makes for a class meeting kind of problem. That year we never got to all the problems in the book, but the children seemed to accept the inevitable postponements.

Question:

At the end of the meeting, do you feel that every problem is resolved?

Answer:

No, and that's okay. I tell the children that real life is not neatly packaged like a TV sitcom that ends in thirty minutes. Life is more complex. Some problems can't be solved in half an hour, and that means that we'll have to revisit them again and again. It's important my students realize that life is not formulaic and trite, and that I am committed to returning to the tougher conflicts we encounter.

Question:

What if no one writes a problem in the notebook?

Answer:

There are two different circumstances when the notebook might remain blank. One happens early in the year, because the children don't know each other very well, and they're on their best behavior. Moreover, they're shy, and worried about being the first ones to write down a problem. I reassure them that it's all right to use the notebook to attempt to resolve problems. I will often praise the first child who has the courage to write in the notebook.

The other circumstance can sometimes occur midway or near the end of the year. It is often a sign that your class is doing well, and that everyone is basically getting along. When that happens I don't cancel the meeting, instead I might discuss why the week went so smoothly. What's different about this week? I might ask. The children then talk about how they're solving their problems more independently, or that the week went by so fast because of some festivity or field trip, and that no one had the time to get into a conflict. This opportunity to reflect about the success of our community during a time of peace and tranquility is important for us. It's nice to be calm, and rejoicing in our new growth.

Sometimes if the notebook is blank, I write a concern or problem I might have noticed in our class, something I've observed about a relationship, perhaps something one of my students is reluctant to write about, such as the time Trevor was being teased for his small size. I wrote in the notebook,

> "I noticed that sometimes children's feelings get hurt when someone calls them by a nickname like 'Shorty,' or 'Lardo,' or any other name that's critical of their size or shape. Has that ever happened to you? Did you hear someone use such language? Let's talk."
>
> — Love, Mona

This direct question made it easier for Trevor to talk about how hurt he had been when some of the boys had called him "Shrimp" during basketball. It had been too scary for Trevor to write down his complaint himself, but my neutral invitation made it possible for him to say to the class he didn't want to be called "Shrimp" anymore.

Other times I use the notebook to ask the children questions about the management of the room, such as the work alone places, or sharing the pillows in our book corner. It gives us a chance to make some decisions together that affect everyone. It's a good introduction to the democratic system.

Question:

What do you do when the problem involves a student from another class, or another adult at the school?

Answer:

Most of the problems written up in the notebook have to do with conflicts that happen between children in our class. However, once in a while a student from a different class gets written up in the notebook. It's often a problem that occurs out in the playground at recess or lunch. When this happens, I first invite the children to talk briefly about the problem so I can figure out what it's about, but I tell them that I'm not comfortable talking about people behind their backs. I urge them to keep our conversation private so it doesn't turn into school gossip. The children understand "gossip," because we spend some time at the beginning of the year discussing the differences between discussing an issue that needs resolving and gossiping about it.

Then I ask the children, "What do you want to do about this problem?" They usually want me to talk to the student's teacher. That's their first choice. Sometimes they want me to help them negotiate the problem one-on-one with that student. Other times they want to write a letter to that student, or invite the student to our class meeting. I explain to the children that it might be hard for a student from a different class to come to one of our class meetings. When I ask why, they are quick to realize that it would be intimidating, and a bit scary to be singled out, and outnumbered.

One time, after repeatedly talking to another teacher at our school about her student, Fanny, and realizing that it wasn't helping, I called a mini-class meeting that involved Fanny's teacher (to support Fanny), Fanny, and the three girls in my class who had constant conflicts with her. The meeting went well. In fact, the three girls in my class were considerate of Fanny's feelings while telling her how hurt they had been by the exclusive kinds of games she played at recess. Fanny's behavior changed some after our talk, but she was still prone to be a bit standoffish with my students. However, what changed was my three students' attitude. Before we had had our mini-class meeting, these girls had been whiny and needy in relation to Fanny. After the meeting the girls seemed less needy, and more empowered, because they were given a chance to feel heard and bolstered. Sometimes that's all the children need.

When the problem written up in the notebook relates to another adult at our school, such as an enrichment teacher, or a lunch supervisor, we follow the same procedures. It's often a little more touchy for me, as I have to maintain a professional relationship with my colleagues while supporting my students. Most of the adults I have had to deal with are agreeable and cooperative, but once in a while I run into awkward situations where the adults might not completely agree with the direct and democratic manner I use to handle these problems. Fortunately, I am lucky to be working in an environment that is cohesive pedagogically, and where most teachers treat children with the same respect and attention I give to my students.

Question:

What if the problem written up in the notebook is a private family matter, or a matter that doesn't pertain to school life?

Answer:

Early on in the year I explain that class meetings are for school matters. Most children understand the boundaries I set with clarity at the beginning of the year. However, there's always a student who doesn't understand these limits, or who might feel so overwhelmed with home issues that they splash over into our midst.

The best way to deal with this is to speak to the child privately. That's another reason I like to review the problems before we have our meetings. If a problem seems too personal for the group, I address it directly with the child, and might ask another teacher, or my administrator for support.

Sometimes the issue is not written up in the notebook, but rears up during the meeting, such as in Pasong's case. Little did I know when I began that class meeting that I was going to contend with issues of molestation and child abuse. Of course, I did what I could at the time, and perhaps if the situation were to come up now in my teaching career, I might deal with it differently. Working with children is not like working with commodities that are constant, like fabric that you cut and sew, or wood that you nail together. Working with children involves the individual child's make-up, your own and the situation at hand. It is highly subjective and interrelational. Sometimes you just try to do the best you can considering the circumstances.

Question:

What do you do when the same problem keeps coming up over and over?

Answer:

If you are teaching elementary school, you know that the world of young children is complex, and that to a certain extent, life with children involves repetition, and that children will be children. The problems of teasing and taunting are an intrinsic part of growing up. You don't have to have a degree in cultural anthropology to recognize the six syllables, "Nah, nah, nah, nah, nah, nah," that are uttered in a singsong voice by children all over the globe. You know what they mean. Childhood teasing crosses the boundaries of gender, language, race and culture.

When a problem comes up for the second or third time in the class notebook, I bring it up to the children, "I've noticed this problem is coming up a lot. Have you noticed that, too?" The children are uncannily aware of the frequency of a problem. Then I ask, "Why do you think this problem is coming up so much?" By talking about it together, I help the children verbalize their insights and theories, "Maybe he can't use his self-control," or they might say, "Maybe she needs a self-governing contract to help her stop what she's doing."

By addressing the situation head-on, we are letting the writer of the problem know we've noticed that something is not working. Talking openly allows us to let the writer know that he is seen and heard. If he needs help, we're here to provide it for him. If he's writing the problem, not because he is repeatedly the victim of some taunting bully, but because he needs to be the center of our attention, we'll help him see what he is doing, and give him the attention he needs via an appropriate channel. A good rule to go by, is to ask myself, what is this child really trying to say to us? What is he or she writing between the lines?

Question:

What do you do about the squirmy child who can't sit still during class meeting?

Answer:

First of all, I try to keep our class meetings to a minimum of thirty minutes and a maximum of forty-five. I think that's a reasonable amount of time on the rug for children who are seven through ten years old. Teachers have to decide what is best for them depending on the age and maturity of their group.

Second, I start our meeting by reminding the children to look at their neighbors on the rug to see if they're sitting next to a special friend with whom they might get distracted. At that moment some children choose to move to a different spot on the rug, and I make sure to praise them for knowing themselves well, and for showing self-control. It's important to acknowledge these things publicly. I tell them that if they want to be in charge of their whereabouts on the rug, they need to make good decisions. I explain that if later on during the meeting, they're being disruptive, I'll have to ask them to move to a different spot without warning them or consulting with them. That means they've forfeited having self-control, and I'll be the one with all the control over them. This early reminder is often all I need to say.

In every classroom at class meeting you can count on having one or more squirmy students. They have a hard time sitting still. They fidget; they touch people and objects around them; they tap, drum, hum, scoot, spin, slouch. The first thing to do is to ask yourself how much tolerance you have for this kind of behavior. Earlier in my career, I used to be less tolerant. I used to "pester" children all the time, remind them, reprimand them, ask them to move to a different area. What I did was disruptive to the flow of the meetings, but I needed then to have all the control. However, now I let some things slide down the wayside. The bottom line is, "Is this child bothering someone else?" If he's not, I let him be. A little bit of squirminess isn't the end of the world.

On the other hand, if he is disturbing someone, I ask him gently to stop what he's doing, and find a different spot at our circle. One year I remember a student who had a hard time sitting without support for his spine. Manuel would start class meetings on the left side of the circle, and unbeknownst to me end up on the right. He seemed to swim, or slither across the rug with the greatest of ease. Most of the time it didn't disturb his classmates, but when it did, I offered him matter-of-factly a chair at our circle which he gladly accepted without feeling punished. I just said to everyone, "A chair helps give Manuel's back some support." And to avoid having all twenty children ask for a chair, I added, "Manuel needs that, and if ever you need something special, I'll make sure you get it." They slowly learned that they didn't need to have everything dished out evenly in class to make it fair, but that I'll support their personal needs when they come up individually.

Question:

What do you do about the quiet child who doesn't participate during class meeting?

Answer:

Just as every classroom has squirmy students, every classroom has quiet ones. In a society that condones and admires the outspoken, vivacious types, it's difficult to gain respect and appreciation for being shy and reserved. My responsibility is not to change my students' personalities and temperaments. I respect my quieter students, and yet I want to offer them a venue of expression at class meetings.

One way I have found that helps everyone participate at class meetings, is when I ask my students general questions to get a hand count, such as "How many people have ever been teased in this class?" "How many people have never been teased?" or "How many kids have felt lonely at lunch?" and "How many people never feel lonely at lunch?" When I ask such questions, everyone is invited to raise a hand, and everyone does, even the shy, reluctant children who might not have answered these questions directly. The children know I won't ask for stories or examples from them to share, it's just a hand-count that makes us all feel part of a group. Then I proceed to count the hands in order to acknowledge the children, and give them a sense of how many people feel the same way they do. I sometimes ask the children to look around at all the raised hands that stand as silent, yet powerful testimonial of support. "You see, you're not alone, all these people feel the same way you do." And other times the message is reversed, "Look around, not too many people have had that experience. Maybe that's why you feel so alone and misunderstood."

Another way I try to be sensitive to the quieter students in my class, is to stop before calling on someone, and say, "Has there been anyone in the group who hasn't had a chance to make a comment yet, and would like to make one now?" By giving the opportunity to the less verbal student to have a voice at our meeting, I teach all the children to become aware of everyone else in our class, even the quiet ones.

Question:

What about the child who monopolizes the meeting?

Answer:

Yes, there are children who monopolize meetings, just as we know adults who monopolize meetings. These children raise their hands all the time. They want to talk all the time. Some of them are mature and have a great deal to contribute to the group, while others have very little of substance to say, or tend to take us away from the issue at hand to a tangent of their choice. These monopolizing children crave the attention of the group.

When I realize we have a persistently monopolizing student in our class, I might write up in the notebook,

> "I noticed that some people talk a lot at class meetings, while others don't as much. Have you noticed that, too? What do you think might be the reason? How can we help kids feel comfortable with the amount of time they participate in the group? Let's talk about it."
>
> — Love, Mona

If this discussion alone doesn't help the talkative children become aware of their role at the meetings, I will talk to them privately. I might ask them to notice how many times their hands are raised during the meeting. I might ask them to keep count on a piece of paper. It's important they become more aware of the group dynamics, and their effect on the group. This exercise is invaluable in helping children move away from egocentric thinking in the social context of our meeting, to a more aware and empathic attitude toward the group.

There's also the talkative student who might not monopolize the meeting by raising a hand at every junction of the conversation, but who instead, might enjoy telling long, elaborate stories in minute details. I had always tried pointing out to these talkers that other students have their hands up, and are patiently waiting for their turn, but it never seemed to be effective. Once these incessant talkers began spinning their tales, they forgot there were other hands in the air.

One year I had such a student, Tamika. She was liked by everyone, but her stories had no end. Usually when I saw her hand go up at our meetings, I dreaded calling on her in fear that we'd be spending the whole day on the rug. Fortunately for me, one day Tamika, herself, gave me the solution to the problem. As she began her long-winded story, I interrupted her to say we only had two minutes left before it was lunch. Her eyes grew big and wide, and she said in a matter-of-fact voice, "Oh, then let me tell you the shorter version." I couldn't believe there had always been a shorter version while we sat there patiently listening to the longer one!

From that day on, Tamika's suggestion enabled me to guide my talkative students toward the shortened version of their stories. Now when we are running out of time, I often interject, "Could you give us the shorter version?" and the children seem to understand, and gladly oblige.

Question:

What is the ideal group size for class meetings?

Answer:

It makes sense that the smaller the number of children, the more intimate the meeting. However, number is not everything. I've facilitated class meetings with small groups of fifteen to twenty children, as well as large groups of thirty. It's more challenging with a larger group, because there are more children who want to talk, but it can be done.

Question:

Have you done class meetings with different ethnic or socioeconomic communities than your own?

Answer:

Yes, I have, and they were important growing experiences for me and for the teachers with whom I worked. A few years ago I met Mrs. Brown and her class. Mrs. Brown taught fourth grade in an inner-city school in Oakland. We met when she attended one of my class meetings workshops, and was eager to begin her own. She asked me if I'd like to visit her classroom, and because I didn't have much experience with inner-city settings, I gladly accepted. After my first visit, I immediately knew I wanted to work with Mrs. Brown. She was a large, warm African-American woman, in her late fifties, with sparkling eyes behind round metal-rimmed glasses. But what I liked most about her was her eagerness to try out new things and her loud infectious laughter.

We both agreed that I would spend the year training her on a weekly basis. The first five months of the year I did the class meetings while she watched and took notes. The second part of the year, she did the class meetings while I observed her. We spent about fifteen minutes debriefing after the meetings while her students had recess.

Mrs. Brown, or Beverly, as I learned to call her, had a class of thirty-one lively fourth graders. They were crammed into a small portable building. Since there was no rug, or cozy spot for class meetings, every Thursday afternoon, when I visited, the children moved all the desks to the back of the room, and we set the chairs in a circle.

What started out as curiosity and eagerness on our respective parts to learn about each other and our teaching methods, became one of the richest experiences—a journey that helped me grow as a teacher, and as a human being. Beverly's students had problems. Many of them couldn't read or write beyond the first-grade level. Twenty-six of them were African-American, three were Asian, and two were White. The children's personal lives were burdened with many of the aches of our society—poverty, parents in jail or on drugs, child abuse, foster care and homelessness.

Beverly's style was very different from mine. She spoke to the children in a stern, dictatorial voice giving them less leeway than I do my students. Yet, they adored her, and I slowly began to appreciate her ways. She once told me, "That's what these kids know, and that's what they respond to the best."

I worried that Beverly's students were going to eat me alive. However, I began doing class meetings in my own way, talking to the children as though I were talking to my own adult friends, and interestingly, they responded to me, and accepted my authority.

The children looked forward to my visits when we could talk about the problems on the playground, their anger, the importance of the media and popular culture in their lives. When Beverly herself started doing class meetings, her voice boomed loudly, and she held the reins tightly. But as the months went by, I one day realized that her voice was less commanding, and that she was sharing episodes from her own childhood with her students. Her warmth became accessible to the children as they became an intimate community. She didn't have to reprimand them. They were completely attentive and involved, because the meeting was the time in the week when their issues were discussed, and when school became relevant to their lives.

Question:

For what age level are class meetings best suited?

Answer:

Class meetings work best with children from seven and up, because starting around that age most children begin to have the ability to listen to other people's perspectives, and can remain focused for a lengthy discussion. In addition, children under seven have needs of their own, such as the need for immediate intervention, and the need for support to resolve their conflicts. And because younger children live in the present, it would be taxing for them to write down a problem in the class notebook, and have to wait a week before resolving it, notwithstanding the actual demanding motor and literacy task of putting down the words on paper.

I have seen teachers of first grade facilitate class meetings by adapting my model to make it suit the needs of younger children. One thing that helped was having shorter meetings of 15 to 20 minutes. A creative first-grade teacher liked observing the issues that came up spontaneously during the week in her class. Then at class meeting she would bring up a concern she observed during the week without confronting the particular children, but more as a general issue. She sometimes read a book about friendship, or teasing or bullying, in order to help the children discuss some of the conflicts and concerns they had in class.

At the other extreme, when I facilitated meetings in a sixth-grade self-contained class, I suggested the teacher share the facilitator's role with his students. Interestingly, the students didn't want the added responsibility. Their most pressing concern was how to remain fair in the face of their friends' conflicts, and how to navigate their allegiances. They felt the role of facilitator would be too burdensome.

Question:

What about students in middle school or high school?

Answer:

It is evident with all the tensions and violence in middle schools and high schools that preteens and teens need the opportunity to discuss their social issues. However, what makes it problematic is these students are not in self-contained classrooms anymore, and their school settings are often very large.

Several years ago at the International Conference on Teacher Research which took place at the University of California at Davis, I met some high school social studies teachers who were experimenting with designing class meetings for their students. Because I had only had the experience of working with elementary-age children, it was interesting to hear these teachers report that their adolescent students preferred discussing their problems anonymously, because the topics of discussion were often more explosive in nature. Therefore, in order to give her students the privacy they needed to discuss issues like, drug and alcohol abuse, sex, sexually transmitted diseases, violence and pregnancy, one teacher placed a "Suggestions for Discussion" box in her classroom. Once a week she used up one of her social studies period to read the topics in the box, and discuss them with her class. She added that, because the discussions were often heated, she had attended a group-facilitating workshop to help her develop the protocols and safe boundaries she needed in order to successfully facilitate her class meetings.

Question:

What mechanism do you use to keep an individual child from feeling scapegoated or picked on by the group?

Answer:

My responsibility as a facilitator of class meetings is to create an environment that fosters trust and safety. I implement class meetings in order to create community and a safe place to learn. However, some teachers or parents fear that a student might be repeatedly picked on during class meeting.

At class meetings it is my role to help children express their grievances in a respectful manner, while at the same time becoming aware of the effects of their words on other children. I'm not claiming that it's quick or easy. It's a process that takes time and commitment, just as it takes time and commitment to teach any other subject. As teachers, we don't give up on the students who struggle and don't understand, for example, that multiplication is a form of repeated addition. Instead, we give them many opportunities to practice and learn from their mistakes and to work in partnership with students who understand the concept and who help them learn by modeling and scaffolding.

What children learn during class meetings takes a lifetime to understand, and in elementary school, they're only at the beginning of that learning continuum. When I notice that some students in my classroom are having difficulties getting along with others, I try, on the one hand, to model to the class how to respond to such students, and on the other hand, I help the challenging students see the effects of their own behaviors. It's often difficult for them to change the antisocial patterns in which they've become stuck.

The best way to illustrate these two methods is with examples from my classroom. In this first example, I modeled for the children a way to handle uncertainty and giving second chances.

- When Sasha had repeatedly teased Lizzie, but denied any responsibility, I told the children that when I can't figure out whether someone is doing something on purpose or if it's an accident, I first trust people. I give them another chance. But if I have another problem with them, then the trust is broken, and I start doubting them. Lizzie listened carefully to my personal wisdom, and gave Sasha a second chance. But a week later, four children witnessed Sasha tricking Lizzie on the swings, and by the time we had a class meeting, Lizzie's trust in Sasha was broken

In such a situation, it is best to have Sasha deal with the logical consequences of her actions. No one picked on her, on the contrary, she was given a second chance, but she blew it. I do not try to protect children like Sasha. It's important they start to be accountable for their actions. One of my responsibilities as a teacher is to make sure all the children in my care feel safe at school. Sasha was making it unsafe for Lizzie. I will not allow anyone to break the trust I am trying to establish in the class. Sasha learned that there are consequences to her actions, and that she couldn't hide from her actions. I think our class meetings saved her from becoming a first class bully.

This second example illustrates the power a classroom teacher has in helping a child change his bad reputation.

- Noah came to third grade hating school. He spent the preceding year in innumerable conflicts, and didn't feel he had any friends. He quickly became a perfect target—the typical challenging student who rubs people the wrong way. The first problem of the year in the notebook was written by Sarah who accused Noah of talking too much at the table, and disturbing everyone.

Noah started out by systematically denying every single thing Sarah said. He hadn't done anything bad, he said. Then as we continued to talk, his story changed a bit, because now he couldn't remember what had happened. As we continued to discuss Sarah's concerns, while giving Noah all the benefit of our doubt, Noah admitted, in passing, that he had, indeed, talked a bit at his table.

At that moment I stopped and praised Noah for his courage to tell the truth. He became slightly self-conscious, but from the grin on his face, I could tell he was proud, too.

Even though this incident seems benign, it was the beginning of a turnaround for Noah. From that day on, whenever someone did something brave in our class, we'd say, "So and so is brave like Noah." Noah, the boy who came to third grade with a chip on his shoulder, the boy who couldn't make friends, was suddenly seen as a valued member of the community, someone the teacher praised, someone to look up to.

This is not to say that Noah suddenly turned angelic. He continued to have his issues and struggles, but something shifted for him. Once I had found some merit in his actions, and the class was a witness to his bravery, he couldn't remain the same. He saw himself change in the eyes of his classmates, and so he began to change himself, too.

Noah would have been picked on all year had he stayed on the periphery of our class, and not become a member of our community. But I pointed out his courage to tell the truth, and slowly his reputation changed. We might not realize it, but we hold a tremendous power over the children we teach. I continued to work with Noah on learning how to become a better friend, and by the end of the year, he began to enjoy school, and make friends.

Question:

Do you allow observers at your class meetings?

Answer:

It depends. If the observers are other educators who are interested in acquiring skills in the art of facilitating class meetings, I invite them to observe the meeting, as long as they can remain inconspicuous, and are willing to debrief and share their observations with me after the meeting.

I make sure to introduce the observers to the children, and I explain the purpose of their visit. It's important the children don't feel anxious because someone is watching and taking notes.

I do not allow parents to observe our class meetings, because the children need a safe and private place away from their parents' eyes to discuss their school social lives. I also know, because I'm a parent myself, that it is very difficult to relinquish our parental investment in our own children in order to observe them objectively and with impartiality.

Question:

What do you do when students use the notebook to threaten their classmates or tattle on them?

Answer:

Early in the year, I like to do a little skit in front of my class. I call it "The Threat of the Notebook". I pretend to be a student who is threatening another child with the notebook. I might say something like, "Well, if you don't stop calling me names, I'm going to write you up in the notebook!" A colleague of mine usually plays the part of the taunting disagreeable child who might be saying forcefully, "But I didn't do anything!" or "I don't care!"

While playing the part of the tattling child who isn't capable of solving her own conflict, but who, instead, exacerbates the problem by being uncooperative, and manipulative, I occasionally stop my performance to ask my students to give me ideas on how to resolve the problem. This opportunity to do things differently is important to children, because it offers them different views and perspectives. They begin to see that there are many different ways to handle a social situation, and that some of the ways are not productive, but can become, in fact, antisocial.

When later in the year, students use the notebook in a manipulative manner, I remind them of my skit, and we discuss the short-lived power and triumph of threatening a classmate.

Question:

Can anyone do class meetings? How much training, if any, does one need?

Answer:

It's important to get some training in class meetings before embarking on such an endeavor because facilitating class meetings takes a lot of skill. As a teacher you have to be willing and committed to explore the world of children's relationships. You need the patience to go over the same problems week after week without getting frustrated and defeated. And you need the discipline to keep in mind the ultimate goals of class meetings (conflict resolution, empathy, community-building), otherwise you can get easily bogged down by the weekly mundane hurdles you will encounter.

It's also important to have some understanding of child development in order to help the children at their particular stage of development. You don't want to hurry a child who might be too young to understand the viewpoint of others while neglecting to prod another child who is ready to take more responsibility. You also need to keep in mind the fidgetiness and attention level of your younger students as you plan for the length of time for your meetings.

It's critical to have the support of another professional while doing class meetings. You might ask another teacher to observe your meetings, and spend some time debriefing with you afterward. To have the observations of another teacher who is not encumbered by the process of facilitating meetings will be extremely beneficial in establishing a time to reflect and dialogue about your class meetings. The collaboration and reflection you institute will help you focus on your challenging students and prevent you from feeling isolated.

Teacher Testimonial

I remember the support and cherish the memory of Diane Lohman for her lifetime of encouragement and enthusiasm about teaching. Diane had been my master teacher when I was a student receiving my education credential. Over the years we forged a friendship, and several times each year we met over breakfast to share our passions, discoveries, and challenges as teachers and students in the art of teaching.

I am including an essay Diane wrote after we completed a year doing class meetings together. Once a week, Diane kindly opened the doors of her classroom of thirty-one fourth graders and collaborated with me in the class meeting process. The following year Diane died suddenly, mid-year, leaving behind a bereft group of students and colleagues. She was one of the most dedicated and beloved teachers at Marin School in Albany, California.

Diane's Story (June 1997)

"Mona began talking about her class meetings a few years ago. It sparked my interest. I found the idea appealing to me since I believe so wholeheartedly in building a community of learners, resolving conflicts and living and working together in a safe and stimulating environment. I did some reading about the process, but, when I tried to implement it in my classroom, I met with frustration—mine and my students. It was hard to keep everyone involved. We often found ourselves going through prescribed steps and going over and over the same problems. Nothing basic changed. With time being so precious and the demands of the curriculum so great, it simply did not add up. I usually gave up after a few months. There was always a lingering sense, though, that I and my students were missing something.

So this year, when Mona told me about the book she was writing about class meetings, she asked if I would like to have her work with me and my class. I jumped at the chance.

It has been a year of discovery, insight and affirmation. What made this process different from others? What has been the yield of these meetings over time? Those are the questions I wish to address.

At our first class meetings, significant procedures were set in place which helped us define and set a tone for the class meeting. Furniture was moved so that we could all gather in a circle in the reading corner of the room. A special hourglass was placed in the center of the circle. We all were silent for one minute. This gave us a chance to shift gears, reflect, and ready ourselves to be present at the meeting.

A simple process was explained in which the teacher would read the problem written in the class notebook. The writer of the problem and others who may have co-signed would elaborate and share their feelings about it. The person named in the problem would respond giving his or her perspective. The discussion would be opened to the class to share their observations, insights and similar experiences.

Then the magic began. Children came forward with clues about causes of problems, shared experiences, possible responses next time a similar situation might arise. The discussion was often punctuated by questions from Mona which involved the whole class. How many of you have ever had this happen? Who has felt like this before? What have you done when you had a similar experience? This helped everyone stay an active participant. Mona shared a story from her childhood. She named the common thread that had emerged. She affirmed children's courage to share.

Over a period of weeks, I had the delicious privilege of watching Mona at work. How often do we have this opportunity to be an observer and truly see and hear our children? I learned how much goes on in children's lives at school that I really had not known. I was delighted to see some of my quietest students share their concerns and experiences. As well as studying the children, I, of course, was studying Mona in earnest. I would marvel at the rhythm of structure and freedom, individual and whole focus, planned and spontaneous moments. Of course, gnawing at the periphery of my mind was the question, would I ever be able to do this?

I had begun asking a few questions, clarifying situations and sharing some thoughts from the beginning, but after a couple of months, Mona, as every good mother bird does, began to push me out of the nest. It was time to try flying on my own.

Here are some discoveries I've made as I have now undertaken more solo flights. My two basic learnings are: 1. Plan and 2. Let go of the plan.

Mona and I consulted each night before the class meeting and read over the problems that had been written in the notebook. We looked for patterns, common themes, the overriding issue. We took note when a child had been written up many times. Was it time for a self-governing contract? This helped us know where we were heading.

Then there is the reality of the class meeting itself. I was always amazed at how what looked like a fairly straight forward problem would have layers of truth and meaning. It was important to go with what emerged and not hang on to our idea of where things should be going. This is a great learning that comes from a powerful belief in people, in truth, in process.

Another lesson—things are not all neatly tied up in a forty-five minute class meeting period. We do not expect pledges from children about what they have learned and will do from now on. There is a trust in the power of awareness. Something new is added to the equation when we hear another's story, feel another's pain, see a new possibility. In class meetings we celebrate the new patterns and insights that have unfolded as a result of previous meetings.

So what has been the yield of this experiment? Children have learned to take more responsibility and show more confidence in solving problems.

They increasingly solve problems on their own and use class meetings for problems that require more help. By seeing the process modeled weekly, they know there are various perspectives in any situation. The more clearly they can define their perspective and feelings about a situation, the more likely they are to be heard.

Often discussions about a particular problem have led to deeper issues children face at this age. Friendship has been a major topic. We have discussed making new friends, disengaging from difficult friendships, choosing friends. Children hear each other and verify that their concerns and experiences are similar. Through this sharing we have developed empathy for each other. Children's play and work take on a more thoughtful and kinder quality.

More individual responsibility in many areas has also been a welcomed outcome of this process. After our first student began his self-governing contract to change his behavior at recess, and had great success, Mona explained that in her classroom some children have asked for contracts to help them reinforce new patterns. Since then two children have asked for a contract, one to increase paying attention to instruction in class, the other to keep his desk clean. Both have met with success and feel more confident in these areas. The rest of the students have shown support and encouragement to those with contracts. They know that when each student succeeds, we all win.

For myself I have learned to listen more carefully, trust my intuition, ask for help. When in a class meeting Mona and I feel stuck and don't quite know where to go, we will say that, and ask the children what they see. Inevitably something emerges which helps us unravel the problem and see a new possibility. I have learned to share more of my own life with the children. They know stories about my experience in fourth grade. I am more real to them. They see that I am learning new things. I have shared with them my fears as I have been learning how to lead class meetings. What I find is the more genuine I can be about what I am experiencing, the freer they feel to share their experiences and insights. This has contributed to the sense that we are there for each other as we fully engage in this brimming, bountiful experience of school life."

References

d'Ortoli, F. & Amram. (1990). M. *L'ecole avec Francoise Dolto*. Paris: Hatier.

Nelsen, Jane, Lott, Lynn, and Glenn, H. Stephen. (1993). *Positive Discipline in the Classroom*. Rocklin, California: Prima Publishing.

Gibbs, Jeanne B. (1987). *Tribes: A Process for Social Development and Cooperative Learning* (rev. ed.). Santa Rosa, California: Center Source Publications.

Glasser, William. (1992). *The Quality School: Managing Students Without Coercion*. (2nd ed.) New York: HarperCollins Publishers.

Paterson, Katherine. (1995). *A Sense of Wonder: On Reading and Writing Books for Children*. New York: Penguin Books.

Suggested Reading List

Coles, Robert. (1990). *The Spiritual Life of Children*. Boston: Houghton-Mifflin Company.

DeVries, R. & Zan, B. (1994). *Moral Classrooms, Moral Children: Creating a Constructivist Atmosphere in Early Education*. New York: Teachers College Press.

Dewey, John. (1916). *Democracy and Edcuation*. New York: The MacMillan Company.

Duckworth, E. (1987). *"The Having of Wonderful Ideas": and Other Essays on Teaching and Learning*. New York: Teachers College Press.

Eisenberg, N. and Mussen, P. (1989). *The Roots of Prosocial Behavior in Children*. Cambridge: Cambridge University Press.

Erikson, Erik. (1963). *Childhood and Society* (2nd ed.) New York: W.W. Norton and Company.

Field, K., Cohler, B., Wool, G. (1989). *Learning and Education: Psychoanalytic Perspectives*. Connecticut: International Universities Press.

Goleman, D. (1995). *Emotional Intelligence*. New York: Bantam Books.

Greenspan, Stanley with Salmon, Jacqueline. (1993). *Playground Politics: Understanding the Emotional Life of Your Child*. Reading, Massachusetts: Addison-Wesley Publishing.

Griffin, E. *Island of Childhood*. (1982). New York: Teachers College Press.

Kohlberg, L. (1981). *The Philosophy of Moral Development: Moral Stages and the Idea of Justice*. San Francisco: Harper & Row.

Lickona, T. (1991). *Educating for Character: How Our Schools Can Teach Respect and Responsibility*. New York: Bantam Books.

Noddings, N. (1992). *The Challenge to Care in Schools*. New York: Teachers College Press.

Piaget, J. (1965). *The Moral Judgment of the Child*. New York: Free Press.

Rogers, C. & Freiberg, H. J. (1994). *Freedom to Learn*. New York: MacMillan College Publishing Company.

Rubin, Zick. (1980). *Children's Friendships*. Cambridge, Massachusetts: Harvard University Press.

Turiel, E. (1983). *The Development of Social Knowledge: Morality and Convention*. New York: Cambridge University Press.

Wadsworth, B. J. (1989). *Piaget's Theory of Cognitive and Affective Development*. (4th ed.). New York: Longman.